Bloom's

GUIDES

Aldous Huxley's
Brave
New World

CURRENTLY AVAILABLE

1984
All the Pretty Horses
Beloved
Brave New World
Cry, the Beloved Country
Death of a Salesman
Hamlet
The Handmaid's Tale
The House on Mango Street
I Know Why the Caged Bird Sings
The Scarlet Letter
To Kill a Mockingbird

Bloom's
GUIDES

Aldous Huxley's
Brave
New World

Edited & with an Introduction
by Harold Bloom

CHELSEA HOUSE
P U B L I S H E R S
An imprint of Infobase Publishing

Bloom's Guides: Brave New World

Copyright © 2004 by Infobase Publishing
Introduction © 2004 by Harold Bloom

Chelsea House
An imprint of Infobase Publishing
132 West 31st Street
New York NY 10001

Library of Congress Cataloging-in-Publication Data
Applied For

ISBN: 0-7910-7566-4

Chelsea House books are available at special discounts when purchased in bulk quantities for businesses, associations, institutions, or sales promotions. Please call our Special Sales Department in New York at (212) 967-8800 or (800) 322-8755.

You can find Chelsea House on the World Wide Web at
http://www.chelseahouse.com

Contributing editor: Aislinn Goodman
Cover design by Takeshi Takahashi

Printed in the United States of America

Bang EJB 10 9 8 7 6 5 4 3 2

This book is printed on acid-free paper.

Contents

Introduction

HAROLD BLOOM

In his "Foreword" to a 1946 edition of *Brave New World* (1931), Aldous Huxley expressed a certain regret that he had written the book when he was an amused, skeptical aesthete rather than the transcendental visionary he had since become. Fifteen years had brought about a world in which there were "only nationalistic radicals of the right and nationalistic radicals of the left," and Huxley surveyed a Europe in ruins after the completion of the Second World War. Huxley himself had found refuge in what he always was to call "the Perennial Philosophy," the religion that is "the conscious and intelligent pursuit of man's Final End, the unitive knowledge of the immanent Tao or Logos, the transcendent godhead or Brahman." As he sadly remarked, he had given his protagonist, the Savage, only two alternatives: to go on living in the Brave New World whose God is Ford (Henry), or to retreat to a primitive Indian village, more human in some ways, but just as lunatic in others. The poor Savage whips himself into the spiritual frenzy that culminates with his hanging himself. Despite Huxley's literary remorse, it seems to me just as well that the book does not end with the Savage saving himself through a mystical contemplation that murmurs "That are Thou" to the Ground of All Being.

A half-century after Huxley's "Foreword," *Brave New World* is at once a bit threadbare, considered strictly as a novel, and more relevant than ever in the era of genetic engineering, virtual reality, and the computer hypertext. Cyberpunk science fiction has nothing to match Huxley's outrageous inventions, and his sexual prophecies have been largely fulfilled. Whether the Third Wave of a Gingrichian future will differ much from Huxley's *Brave New World* seems dubious to me. A new technology founded almost entirely upon information rather than production, at least for the elite, allies Mustapha Mond and Newt Gingrich, whose orphanages doubtless can be geared to the bringing up of Huxley's "Bokanovsky groups." Even Huxley's intimation that "marriage licenses will be sold like dog licenses, good for a period of twelve months," was being seriously considered in California not so long ago. It is true that Huxley expected (and feared) too much from the "peaceful" uses of atomic energy, but that is one of his few failures in secular prophecy. The God of the Christian Coalition may not exactly be Our Ford, but he certainly is the God whose worship assures the world without end of Big Business.

Rereading *Brave New World* for the first time in several decades, I find myself most beguiled by the Savage's passion for Shakespeare, who provides the novel with much more than its title. Huxley, with his own passion for Shakespeare, would not have conceded that Shakespeare could have provided the Savage with an alternative to a choice between an insane utopia and a barbaric lunacy. Doubtless, no one ever has been saved by reading Shakespeare, or by watching him performed, but Shakespeare, more than any other writer, offers a possible wisdom, as well as an education in irony and the powers of language. Huxley wanted his Savage to be a victim or scapegoat, quite possibly for reasons that Huxley himself never understood. *Brave New World*, like Huxley's earlier and better novels *Antic Hay* and *Point Counter Point*, is still a vision of T. S. Eliot's *Waste Land*, of a world without authentic belief and spiritual values. The author of *Heaven and Hell* and the anthologist of *The Perennial Philosophy* is latent in *Brave New World*, whose Savage dies in order to help persuade Huxley himself that he needs a reconciliation with the mystical Ground of All Being.

Biographical Sketch

Aldous Leonard Huxley was born on July 6, 1894, in Godalming in Surrey, England. He came from a family of distinguished scientists and writers: his grandfather was Thomas Henry Huxley, the great proponent of evolution, and his brother was Julian Sorrell Huxley, who became a leading biologist. Aldous attended the Hillside School in Godalming and then entered Eton in 1908, but he was forced to leave in 1910 when he developed a serious eye disease that left him temporarily blind. In 1913 he partially regained his sight and entered Balliol College, Oxford.

Around 1915 Huxley became associated with a circle of writers and intellectuals who gathered at Lady Ottoline Morell's home, Garsington Manor House, near Oxford; here he met T. S. Eliot, Bertrand Russell, Osbert Sitwell, and other figures. After working briefly in the War Office, Huxley graduated from Balliol in 1918 and the next year began teaching at Eton. He was, however, not a success there and decided to become a journalist. Moving to London with his wife Maria Nys, a Belgian refugee whom he had met at Garsington and married in 1919, Huxley wrote articles and reviews for the *Athenaeum* under the pseudonym Autolycus.

Huxley's first two volumes were collections of poetry, but it was his early novels—*Crome Yellow* (1921), *Antic Hay* (1923), and *Those Barren Leaves* (1925)—that brought him to prominence. By 1925 he had also published three volumes of short stories and two volumes of essays. In 1923 Huxley and his wife and son moved to Europe, where they traveled widely in France, Spain, and Italy. A journey around the world in 1925–26 led to the travel book *Jesting Pilate* (1926), just as a later trip to Central America produced *Beyond the Mexique Bay* (1934). *Point Counter Point* (1928) was hailed as a landmark in its incorporation of musical devices into the novel form. Huxley developed a friendship with D. H. Lawrence, and from 1926 until Lawrence's death in 1930 Huxley spent much time looking after him during his illness with tuberculosis; in 1932 he edited Lawrence's letters.

In 1930 Huxley purchased a small house in Sanary, in southern France. It was here that he wrote one of his most celebrated volumes, *Brave New World* (1932), a negative utopia or "dystopia" that depicted a nightmarish vision of the future in which science and technology are used to suppress human freedom.

Huxley became increasingly concerned about the state of civilization as Europe lurched toward war in the later 1930s: he openly espoused pacifism and (in part through the influence of his friend Gerald Heard) grew increasingly interested in mysticism and Eastern philosophy. These tendencies were augmented when he moved to southern California in 1937. With Heard and Christopher Isherwood, Huxley formed the Vedanta Society of Southern California, and his philosophy was embodied in such volumes as *The Perennial Philosophy* (1945) and *Heaven and Hell* (1956).

During World War II Huxley worked as a scenarist in Hollywood, writing the screenplays for such notable films as *Pride and Prejudice* (1941) and *Jane Eyre* (1944). This experience led directly to Huxley's second futuristic novel, *Ape and Essence* (1948), a misanthropic portrait of a post-holocaust society written in the form of a screenplay.

In California Huxley associated with Buddhist and Hindu groups, and in the 1950s he experimented with hallucinogenic drugs such as LSD and mescalin, which he wrote about in *The Doors of Perception* (1954). *Brave New World Revisited* (1958), a brief treatise that discusses some of the implications of his earlier novel, continues to be very pessimistic about the future society, particularly in the matters of overpopulation and the threat of totalitarianism. But in *Island* (1962)—the manuscript of which Huxley managed to save when a brush fire destroyed his home and many of his papers in 1961—he presents a positive utopia in which spirituality is developed in conjunction with technology.

Late in life Huxley received many honors, including an award from the American Academy of Letters in 1959 and election as a Companion of Literature of the British Royal Society of Literature in 1962. His wife died in 1955, and the next year he married Laura Archera, a concert violinist. Aldous Huxley died of cancer of the tongue on November 22, 1963, the same day as John F. Kennedy and C. S. Lewis.

The Story Behind the Story

Aldous Huxley's decision to merge science with literature seems an obvious choice when one considers his heritage. Born in 1894 in Surrey, England, Huxley's father, Leonard Huxley, was editor of *Cornhill* magazine, a literary journal that published authors such as George Eliot, Thomas Hardy, Alfred, Lord Tennyson and Robert Browning. His mother, Julia Arnold, was the niece of the poet Matthew Arnold, and her sister, Mary Humphrey Ward, was a popular novelist in her own right. Huxley's grandfather was the famous biologist T. H. Huxley, Charles Darwin's disciple and protégé.

As it was proper for the son of two such distinguished intellectual families, Huxley attended Eton with the hopes of following in the footsteps of his grandfather and elder brother Julian by becoming a doctor and scientist. Such dreams were dashed when Huxley was sixteen, as he contracted a serious disease that left him completely blind for two years, and seriously damaged his vision for the rest of his life. Huxley changed career paths and in 1916, received his undergraduate degree in literature from Balliol College, Oxford.

Huxley began writing professionally in 1920 for various magazines, and published his first novel, *Crome Yellow*, in 1920 at the age of twenty-six. His satirical voice was well-received, and went on to publish several more novels, producing *Point Counter Point* in 1928, establishing himself as a best-selling author. Although it has not been Huxley's most enduring novel, many critics believe *Point Counter Point* to be his most ambitious and successful work. It was on the heels of this success that Huxley produced *Brave New World*.

Brave New World sold 13,000 copies in England in its first year, 3000 more than *Point Counter Point*. But although the novel was a success in terms of sales, reviews were uniformly negative. A departure from his previously lively, "carnivalesque" style, critics accused *Brave New World* of being dry, boring, and overly simplistic. His vision of the future was seen as interesting but irrelevant and unoriginal. In his journal *Books*,

M. C. Dawson called the novel "a lugubrious and heavy-handed piece of propaganda." Illustrating the attitude of many reviewers, the following is an excerpt from the *New Statesman and Nation*:

> [T]his squib about the future is a thin little joke, epitomized in the undergraduate jest of a civilization dated A.F., and a people who refer reverently to 'our Ford'—not a bad little joke, and what it lacks in richness Mr. Huxley tries to make up by repetition; but we want rather more to a prophecy than Mr. Huxley gives us ... The fact is Mr. Huxley does not really care for the story—the idea alone excites him. There are brilliant, sardonic little splinters of hate aimed at the degradation he has foreseen for our world; there are passages in which he elaborates conjectures and opinions already familiar to readers of his essays ... There are no surprises in it; and if he had no surprises to give us, why should Mr. Huxley have bothered to turn this essay in indignation into a novel?

The reviewer finds "prophecy" in Huxley's novel, and is disappointed with the simplicity of it. But Huxley insisted that *Brave New World* was not a prophetic novel, but a cautionary one. He saw the rapid changes that scientific advancement was allowing in his society and, aided by a strong scientific background, imagined how much further it might go. In a 1962 interview, Huxley defends his purpose in writing the novel:

> [Technology could] iron [humans] into a kind of uniformity, if you were able to manipulate their genetic background ... if you had a government unscrupulous enough you could do these things without any doubt ... We are getting more and more into a position where these things *can* be achieved. And it's extremely important to realize this, and to take every possible precaution to see they shall *not* be achieved. This, I take it, was the message of the book—*This is possible: for heaven's sake be careful about it.*

Another complaint was Huxley's "preoccupation with sexuality." The promiscuity of Huxley's futuristic society, and the ease with which he discusses it, was shocking and disturbing. A reviewer from London's *Times Literary Supplement* wrote "it is not easy to become interested in the scientifically imagined details of life in this mechanical Utopia. Nor is there compensation in the amount of attention that [Huxley] gives to the abundant sex life of these denatured human beings."

It is also worth noting that Huxley composed *Brave New World* in 1931, when Europe and America were still reeling—economically, politically, and socially—from World War I. Massive industrialization, coupled with severe economic depression and the rise of fascism, were the backdrop for the novel. It was this turbulence that informed Huxley's cautionary vision of the future. But the massive destruction of World War II was yet to be seen, and Huxley's imagined history of the Nine Years' War and the persecution that followed might have seemed a bit fantastical.

A decade later, the strength of fascist states such as Nazi Germany and the Soviet Union, coupled with the terror of World War II, radically changed the world's vision of future possibilities. Huxley's warning of an all-powerful government was more relevant than Mr. Dawson thought in 1932. In the second half of the twentieth century, advances in biology were so vast that a eugenic society became more than a mad Englishman's far-fetched fantasy. And today, with the development of successful experiments in cloning, Huxley's tale of caution has somehow morphed into one of prophecy. Even Huxley, in his introduction to *Brave New World* written in 1946, admits:

> All things considered it looks as though Utopia were far closer to us than anyone, only fifteen years ago, could have imagined. Then, I projected it six hundred years into the future. Today it seems quite possible that the horror may be upon us within a single century ... Indeed, unless we choose to decentralize and to use applied science, not

as the end to which human beings are to be made the means, but as the means to producing a race of free individuals, we have only two alternatives to choose from: either a number of national, militarized totalitarianisms, having as their root the terror of the atomic bomb and as their consequence the destruction of civilization ... or else one supranational totalitarianism, called into existence by the social chaos resulting from rapid technological progress in general and the atomic revolution in particular, and developing, under the need for efficiency and stability, into the welfare-tyranny of Utopia. You pays your money and you takes your choice.

Each decade brings its technological advances, and these advances inexorably alter the social fabric of the world. Perhaps his guesses were simply lucky, but Huxley's Utopia seems closer every day. This ability of *Brave New World* to become *more* relevant as time passes accounts for its continual popularity, both as a period piece and as an ever-modern novel.

List of Characters

The **Director of Hatcheries and Conditioning for Central London** is the head of the Central Hatchery where many of the characters work and much of the narrative takes place. He introduces the reader to the facility and the fundamentals of Huxley's futuristic society. It is the Director's accident while visiting the Savage Reservation years earlier that provides the impetus for the second half of the novel.

Henry Foster is one of Lenina's boyfriends, and accompanies the Director on the student tour of the Central Hatchery and Conditioning Center in the first section of the novel. He serves as a counterpoint to Bernard Marx—where Bernard is anti-social, eccentric, and individual, Henry is the model conditioned citizen.

Lenina Crowne works in the Central Hatchery and Conditioning Centre, and accompanies Bernard to the Savage Reservation in New Mexico. Her beauty attracts John, and she becomes the object of his romantic and possessive love. She serves as the liaison between civilized and savage society, as she feels a strong connection for John but is confused by what seems to be a growing predilection for monogamy and love. John's attraction to her, and her inability to abandon the promiscuous dictates of her conditioning, serves as a major conflict during John's visit to London.

Mustapha Mond is one of ten World Controllers, and his sphere of influence includes England. His position as one of the major upholders of conditioned society is complicated by his understanding of the sacrifice necessary for such a strict society; his secret stash of forbidden religious and literary texts, as well as his personal history as a young man faced with exile or the renunciation of his pursuit of knowledge, demonstrate that individual awareness has not been eradicated in the "civilized" world, but merely suppressed.

Bernard Marx is an example of unsuccessful, or incomplete, conditioning. Perhaps due to an accident of his conditioning while he was still "bottled," Bernard is physically imperfect, melancholy, and dissatisfied with life in London. Rather than regularly taking soma and engaging in state-supervised entertainment, he complains about London's lack of individuality and feels an outsider in a society that purports to abolish self-consciousness. He is responsible for bringing John and Linda to London, and is finally exiled as a result of his predilection for criticism of the state.

Fanny Crowne also works in the Conditioning Centre, and is Lenina's friend. She serves as a warning voice when Lenina exhibits a desire for monogamy, first with Henry Foster and later with John. When Lenina considers the strange passion she feels for John, Fanny counsels her to date and sleep with him, and explains Lenina's surprising depression as evidence that she needs a Violent Passion Surrogate. Like Henry, Fanny is a model citizen, and cannot contemplate behaving against her conditioning.

Helmholtz Watson feels like an outsider in conditioned society. He writes propaganda for several state-sanctioned publications, but longs to write something more meaningful and passionate. He immediately befriends John, and is enthralled by the forbidden writings of Shakespeare (which John reveals to him). Like Bernard, he is ultimately exiled by Mond to the Falkland Islands where he can pose no threat to the stability of conditioned society; unlike Bernard, Helmholtz anticipates his exile as an opportunity to escape the limited society of London and looks forward to having the freedom to explore his individuality in writing.

Linda is the Beta-Minus who accompanies the Director to the Savage Reservation decades before the novel's timeframe. She is lost during a storm and is left in New Mexico, where she is rescued by an Indian tribe. She is pregnant at the time of her accident, and without the availability of London's Abortion

Centres, is forced to viviparously give birth to the son of the Director. She never fully adjusts to uncivilized life, and struggles to adapt her conditioned mind to unconditioned society.

John is the son of Linda and the Director, born on the Savage Reservation. He presents a unique problem, as he is the son (in itself, an abomination) of a conditioned woman who tries to condition him as best she can outside of the technology of London, but is raised in an unconditioned society. The result is John's inability to complete identify or fit into either world. This becomes clear when he accompanies Bernard to London, and is viewed as sideshow entertainment, both fascinating and foreign because of his tendency to form passionate and monogamous attachments to his mother and Lenina. Civilized society has no place for the uncivilized, but neither does the Savage Reservation have a place for someone born to a civilized woman. His lack of place, and therefore lack of identity, is one the major themes of the novel.

Summary and Analysis

The novel opens at the main entrance of the Central London Hatchery and Conditioning Centre, over which reads the motto of the World State: "COMMUNITY, IDENTITY, STABILITY." This echoes in form, yet contradicts in meaning, the motto of the French Revolution: "LIBERTY, EQUALITY, FRATERNITY." Immediately the reader is aware that this story is to be an ironic one, and the world in which it is set is not of the democratic vision fought for in late eighteenth-century France.

The narrative begins as the Director of the Central Hatchery (never named beyond his title) leads a tour of young students through the facility in **chapter 1**. Huxley cleverly allows the reader an introduction to his futuristic world by allowing us to follow the narrative from the perspective of one of these students. The Director conducts us through the whole facility in order to give the students a general idea of the complete process of Hatching and Conditioning; "For of course some sort of general idea they must have, if they were to do their work intelligently—though as little of one, if they were to be good and happy members of society, as possible. For particulars, as every one knows, make for virtue and happiness; generalities are intellectually necessary evils. Not philosophers but fretsawyers and stamp collectors compose the backbone of society."

Huxley uses this tour as a realistic way to introduce the reader to the futuristic world he has created. The story takes place in A.F. 632, corresponding to 2540 A.D. (A.F. standing for a new system of dating which is explained in Chapter 3).

The tour begins in the Fertilizing Room, where the Director outlines the basic method of fertilization. Selected women are paid the equivalent of six-months' salary to undergo an operation in which an ovary is excised and kept "alive and actively developing." As such, the ovary will continue to produce eggs (ova) in its laboratory environment. Each egg is carefully inspected for abnormalities, and if it passes scrutiny it is then placed in a container with several other ova and is immersed in a high concentration of spermatozoa. The eggs remain in the solution until each is fertilized, after which they are all returned to the incubators.

Here Huxley first introduces the idea of the Caste System, seemingly based on the Indian system with which Huxley, as a citizen of the British Empire would be quite familiar. People belong to one of five castes, Alpha being the most respected and Epsilon being the least: Alpha, Beta, Gamma, Delta, or Epsilon (each caste is then divided into three stratums: e.g., Alpha Plus, Alpha, and Alpha Minus). Castes are determined before fertilization; Alpha and Beta ova remain in their incubators until they are "definitely bottled" (explained below), but Gamma, Delta, and Epsilon ova are removed from their incubators so that they may undergo Bokanovsky's Process. "One egg, one embryo, one adult—normality. But a bokanovskified egg will bud, will proliferate, will divide. From eight to ninety-six buds, and every bud will grow into a full-sized adult. Making ninety-six human beings grow where only one grew before." The Director explains to the students (and the reader): "Essentially bokanovskification consists of a series of arrests of development. We check the normal growth and, paradoxically enough, the egg responds by budding." Thus one fertilized egg produces up to ninety-six identical twins.

One student asks the Director what advantage bokanovskification provides. The Director explains that "Bokanovsky's Process is one of the major instruments of social stability!" Ideally the entire working class would be composed of one enormous Bokanovsky Group, giving an unheard-of stability to one's identity, and by extension, to one's society (recall the planetary motto of "COMMUNITY, IDENTITY, STABILITY"). Originally, mass production of twins was hindered only by the "ninety-six buds per ova" limit, but also by the length of time needed by an ovary to produce eggs. At a normal rate of production, an ovary may produce 200 eggs over thirty years, but the goal of mass production is to yield as many identical (or nearly identical) things as possible in the shortest amount of time. Podsnap's Technique, allowing one ovary to produce 150 mature eggs in only two years, quickens the process: "you get an average of nearly eleven thousand brothers and sisters in a hundred and fifty batches of identical twins, all within two years of the same age."

The narrator describes Bokanovsky's Process as logical and rational: "The principle of mass production at last applied to biology." While this statement is not overtly judgmental or even ironic, one must remember Huxley wrote the novel in the early 1930s, just as industrialization was beginning to affect and dominate the average man's life. While it is dangerous to make too many assumptions about an author's undocumented feelings about specific events, it is safe to assume that *any* person living at that time would have been more than a little anxious about the rapidly changing fabric of daily life. It is not difficult to see how an imagination as active as Huxley's was able to take this common anxiety and the rate at which industry was moving toward mass production and imagine the endpoint of such "progress." In many ways, *Brave New World* demonstrates the result of transplanting the growing ideals of mass production onto humanity itself, rather than simply humanity's machines. This is something to keep in mind throughout the novel; the narrator's opinion of the society that he describes becomes more obvious as the story progresses.

The Director introduces Henry Foster to the students, and asks him to explain the record number of production for a single ovary. Henry explains that London's record is 16,012, but that in tropical centers they have reached as high as 17,000. However, he is quick to point out that the "negro ovary" responds much faster to the process. The Director invites Henry to join him in leading the students, and they move on to the Bottling Room.

Huxley describes the Bottling Room as a production line in a factory (indeed, his Hatchery and Conditioning Centre is little more than a factory that produces socialized humans). First, he describes the Liners: a device lifts "flaps of fresh sow's peritoneum ready cut to the proper size" from the Organ Store, and the Liners take each flap and place it on the bottom of a bottle. This is the first step in constructing an artificial womb for the fertilized ova. Next, the Matriculators carefully slit the peritoneal lining, insert the ova, and fill the bottle with a saline solution. Finally, the Labelers tag the bottles with the ova's heredity, date of fertilization, and membership of Bokanovsky Group. "No longer anonymous, but named, identified, the procession marched slowly on into the Social Predestination Room."

The Director, Henry, and the students follow the bottles in the Social Predestination Room, which is a sort of library/research center that determines how many of which caste should be produced at which time. The Social Predestinators control the Decanting Rate, effectively controlling the population. Henry jokes, "If you knew the amount of overtime I had to put in after the last Japanese earthquake!" The Predestinators send their information to the Fertilizers, who then give them the number and caste of embryos requested. After the bottles are "predestined in detail" they are sent to the Embryo Store, the next stop on our tour of the facility.

The Embryo Store is warm and very dark, for as Henry explains to the students, "Embryos are like photographic film ... They can only stand red light." Huxley describes the Store: "And in effect the sultry darkness into which the students now followed him was visible and crimson, like the darkness of closed eyes of a summer afternoon. The bulging flanks of row on receding row and tier above tier of bottles glinted with innumerable rubies, and among the rubies moved the dim red spectres of men and women with purple eyes and all the symptoms of lupus. The hum and rattle of machinery faintly stirred the air." Each bottle was placed on a rack when it arrived from the Social Predestination Room, and each rack was a slow-moving conveyer belt traveling at 33 1/3 centimeters per hour. Various chemicals and hormones are injected into the embryo at specific positions on the conveyer; for example, every embryo is installed with "artificial maternal circulation" at Metre 112, and every bottle is shaken into familiarity with movement during the last two meters of every eight. Each bottle travels exactly 2136 meters before it is decanted, or "born."

This decanting provokes the narrator to make his first overt judgment on the process and society he is describing; embryos are decanted into "Independent existence—so called." Huxley suggests that once an embryo has been created from stock reproductive organs of a certain caste, and then predestined for specific climates, likes and dislikes, and occupations, that "independent existence" has become impossible. The reader is reminded or the irony of the World State's Motto, and realizes the depth of the narrator's ironic judgment.

Henry explains the method of sterilization used in the Embryo Store to the students. Thirty percent of female embryos are allowed to develop normally so that they will mature with a fertile reproductive system. Henry points out that one fertile ovary per 1200 would be sufficient to continue current levels of reproduction. However, thirty percent assures the Hatchery an excellent selection of genetic material. There is no risk of a genetically defective ovary being harvested and used to produce 15,000 ova. The remaining seventy percent of female embryos are injected with male sex-hormone every twenty-four meters, starting at Metre 200. These will become sterile females, or freemartins.

The embryos are conditioned in numerous ways while on the conveyer belts: those destined to become Epsilons and Deltas are given less oxygen, thus stunting their neurological and physical growth. The Director asks the students, "Hasn't it occurred to you than an Epsilon embryo must have an Epsilon environment as well as an Epsilon heredity?" Embryos undergo Heat conditioning, preparing them physically to work in specific latitudes: "Later on their minds would be made to endorse the judgment of their bodies."

Huxley's futuristic society is compelling because it is imperfect; it is still in the throes of scientific investigation, and is still seeking ways to make the reproductive process more efficient. Henry suggests the advantage of producing humans who are completely mature in a shorter timespan, and explains Pilkington's experiments in Mombasa. Pilkington was able to manufacture individuals who were sexually mature at four and physically-mature at six and a half. However he had been unable to speed the mental maturation, so the result was a useless one of adults "too stupid to do even Epsilon work." Henry's tone is one of regret and hopefulness; it is obvious that the discovery of a method to speed maturation would be as significant as Bokanovsky and Podsnap's discoveries.

The tour group comes upon a particularly pretty nurse with whom Henry is acquainted; he introduces the students to Lenina Crowne. Upon Henry's request, Lenina explains that she is injecting embryos with typhoid and sleeping sickness inoculations at Metre 150; these embryos are predestined to work in the tropics, and immunizing them at such an early stage of development insures that they are safe from such tropical diseases. Henry explains to the students, "We immunize the fish against the future man's disease."

After viewing the conditioning of future chemical workers (so that they may tolerate lead, caustic soda, tar, and chlorine) and future rocket-plane engineers (whose bottles are kept in constant rotation to improve their sense of balance), the students begin to head toward the conditioning of Alpha Plus Intellectuals, the highest stratum of the highest caste. In the interest of time, however, the Director prevents the students and the readers from viewing that conditioning, thus denying us the knowledge of such procedures. One recalls his statement above that while one must be given some sort of general idea of the whole, it is dangerous for individuals to focus too much on generalities. Perhaps the students (and by extension, the reader) has been given as much of an overview of fertilization and embryonic development as is safe for their limited intellectual development.

While chapter 1 focuses on the conditioning and development of individual embryos, **chapter 2** moves on to describe the further socialization of decanted human beings. The student tour (leaving Henry Foster in the Decanting Room) proceeds from the Embryo Store to the Infant Nurseries. The first stop is in the Neo-Pavlovian Conditioning Rooms, where infants are conditioned to associate certain objects with fear, thus guaranteeing their dislike of said object throughout their adult life. This method of conditioning draws from the work of Ivan Pavlov, a Russian scientist of the late nineteenth and early twentieth century. Through his study of the behavior of dogs, Pavlov demonstrated the existence of "conditioned reflexes," or responses that seem instinctive to an adult but are actually the result of some previous, repetitive association.

The students follow the Director into a large sunny room in which a handful of nurses are setting out bowls of roses in a long row across the middle of the room. Between each bowl they place "nursery quartos opened invitingly each at some gaily coloured image of beast or fish or bird." Once the roses and books are laid out in a row, the nurses bring in a Bokanovsky Group of eight-month-old Delta babies. The infants are placed on the floor and immediately begin to crawl toward the flowers and books, with "little squeals of excitement, gurgles and twitterings of pleasure." Once all the children are happily engaged with the toys the Head Nurse presses a lever, signaling a shrieking siren and alarm bells. The children are terrified, but the lesson is not complete until it is cemented with electric shock: "[The Director] waved his hand again, and the Head Nurse pressed a second lever. The screaming of the babies suddenly changed its tone. There was something desperate, almost insane, about the sharp spasmodic yelps to which they now gave utterance. Their little bodies twitched and stiffened; their limbs moved jerkily as if to the tug of unseen wires." The Director explains to the students that the Nurse is able to electrify the entire strip of floor. After the alarms and electricity cease, the children are again offered the books and roses, but this time they are terrified by the sight. This exercise will be repeated two hundred times while the infants are in the nursery, forever linking terror and pain with books and flowers. The Director assures the students, "They'll be safe from books and botany all their lives."

The students understand the necessity of conditioning the lower castes to despise books (as too much learning is dangerous), but one boy asks the purpose of adding flowers to the drill. The Director explains that while flowers themselves pose no threat to the individual or the society, they "have one grave defect: they are gratuitous. A love of nature keeps no factories busy." Originally, the lower castes had been conditioned to love flowers and nature so that they would be compelled to consume transport to the country in their free time. However, it was not long before another, more economically sound method was developed to lure the people into consuming mass transport into the country. "We condition the masses to hate the country, but simultaneously we condition them to love all country sports. At the same time, we see to it that all country sports entail the use of elaborate apparatus. So that they consume manufactured articles as well as transport."

The Director changes the subject, telling the students the story of Reuben Rabinovitch, a boy who lived hundreds of years ago in old viviparous days. The students are embarrassed by the thought of viviparous reproduction (i.e., reproduction resulting from sexual contacts between parents), and they have only a partial understanding of "sex," "parents," "birth," and "homes." The Director soothes their embarrassment: "These are unpleasant facts; I know it. But then most historical facts *are* unpleasant ... For you must remember that in those days of gross viviparous reproduction, children were always brought up their parents and not in State Conditioning Centres." The story of Reuben is such: one night his parents accidentally left the radio playing in his bedroom while he slept. The next morning, Polish-speaking Reuben (the Director pauses to remind the students that "Polish," like "French" and "German," is a dead language) was able to recite perfectly, in English, George Bernard Shaw's speech on his own genius, which had been playing on the radio while he slept. Reuben's experience led to the discovery of hypnopaedia, or sleep-teaching.

It took nearly two-hundred years for hypnopaedia to be used officially, because experiments attempted to use it for "intellectual education"; these experiments failed miserably as children would wake up able to recite passages of scientific information, but they were unable to understand the meaning of the recitation. "Quite rightly. You can't learn a science unless you know what it's all about." Hypnopaedia was useless until it was applied to "moral education," which, the Director proclaims, "ought never, in any circumstances, to be rational."

While explaining hypnopaedia to the students, the Director says, "'The case of Little Reuben occurred only twenty-three years after Our Ford's first T-Model was put on the market.' (Here the Director made a sign of the T on his stomach and all the students reverently followed suit.'" This is the novel's first mention of "Ford," and although it seems incongruous, the close reader will infer that the Director speaks of Henry Ford, the American inventor and businessman who founded Ford Motors. Furthermore, the reader may notice the religious symbolism of the "sign of the T" and recall the date offered in chapter 1: A.F. 632. Huxley's society has substituted Henry Ford for Jesus Christ, and the symbol of the T-Model automobile for that of the crucifix, which will be discussed later in this section.

The Director leads the students into another room, a dormitory filled with eighty Beta boys and girls sleeping in cots. The students are instructed to be silent, and they listen to the hypnopaedic lesson ("Elementary Class Consciousness") broadcast from a speaker underneath each child's pillow:

Alpha children wear grey. They work much harder than we do, because they're so frightfully clever. I'm really awfully glad I'm a Beta, because I don't work so hard. And then we are much better than the Gammas and Deltas. Gammas are stupid. They all wear green, and Delta children wear khaki. Oh no, I don't want to play with Delta children. And Epsilons are still worse. They're too stupid to be able to read or write. Besides they wear black, which is such a beastly colour. I'm so glad I'm a Beta.

This lesson will be repeated 120 times per week for thirty months, over 15,000 times in total. Once this lesson is cemented, the children will move on to a more advanced "Class Consciousness" lesson. Furthermore, this is only one of many different lessons hynopaedically taught to the children as they mature. The Director lectures: "Till at last the child's mind *is* these suggestions, and the sum of the suggestions *is* the child's mind. And not the child's mind only. The adult's mind—all his life long. The mind that judges and desires and decides—made up of these suggestions. But all these suggestions are *our* suggestions!"

Chapter 3 is composed of three different stories, all occurring simultaneously within the Hatchery. Each story follows a character and will be referred to as plots 1, 2, and 3 (numbered according to the order in which each plot is introduced). The chapter jumps between the three stories throughout; by the end of the chapter, it is rare that two consecutive sentences follow the same plot. For this summary, I have mapped each plotline as though it were independent, and here I will track each separately. It is important to remember, however, that the stories are happening at the same time. By constantly demonstrating the temporal location of each story in relation to the other two, Huxley is able to draw connections and contrasts between them.

The tour skips to another location, now on the playground outside of the Hatchery in plot 1. Hundreds of children are playing games such as Centrifugal Bumble-puppy, which of course requires a massive amount of apparatus to play, therefore increasing consumption as well as providing entertainment. Many other children, around seven or eight years old, are involved in erotic exploration and "rudimentary sexual games." While in the previous chapter, the students were embarrassed and horrified by the inappropriateness of mothers and fathers, sexual activity that does *not* result in reproduction is acceptable and even encouraged. The students watch a nurse pull a crying young boy out from behind a bush, followed by a concerned young girl. The nurse explains that she is taking the boy to the psychology department because he is reluctant to join in the expected erotic play. The Director comforts the girl, Polly Trotsky, and sends her back to play. The students are astonished when the Director tells them that in Ford's day, erotic play was suppressed among children and young adults.

The group is surprised by the appearance of Mustapha

Mond, the Resident Controller for Western Europe, one of only ten World Controllers. Mond reminds the students of Our Ford's famous saying, "History is bunk," and uses it as support for the World State's refusal to teach anything historical. While Mond speaks of history, the Director worries that he is treading dangerously close to verbalizing blasphemy: "The D.H.C. looked at him nervously. There were those strange rumours of old forbidden books hidden in a safe in the Controller's study. Bibles, poetry—Ford knew what." Intuiting the Director's thoughts, Mond turns to him: "'It's all right Director,' he said in a tone of faint derision, 'I won't corrupt them.'"

Mond shocks the students by forcing them to imagine what it must have been like "to have a viviparous mother." He explains the meaning of the word "home" as "a few small rooms, stiflingly over-inhabited ... No air, no space; an understerilized prison; darkness, disease, and smells ... (The Controller's evocation was so vivid that one of the boys, more sensitive than the rest, turned pale at the mere description and was on the point of being sick.)" He describes a "mother" as a cat: "The mother brooded over her children (*her* children) ... brooded over them like a cat over its kittens; but a cat that could talk, a cat that could say, 'My baby, my baby,' over and over again."

The Controller then speaks of "our Freud, as for some inscrutable reason, [Ford] chose to call himself whenever he spoke of psychological matters—Our Freud had been the first to reveal the appalling dangers of family life." It appears that in the zealous repudiation of history, even the identity of Henry Ford, their savior, has been confused with a nineteenth-century psychologist.

"... Husbands, wives, lovers. There were also monogamy and romance." The students are unfamiliar with any of these terms, and are confused because they have been hypnopaedically instructed that "every one belongs to everyone else." (chapter 3, and the remainder of the novel, is peppered with hypnopaedic proverbs, sometimes identified but often simply a part of a character's vocabulary. These sayings are always short, and often have the sound of children's nursery rhyme. Above all, they are instructive in meaning, neat in form, and easy to remember.) This lack of ownership, Mond explains, allows an infinite number of outlets for emotions, effectively reducing the magnitude of any one feeling. He uses the image of pressurized water in a pipe, and the magnitude of the jet of water if the pipe is pierced once, versus the "piddling little fountains" if it is pierced twenty times. The problem with the "pre-moderns" (Huxley's own society, and our modern world) was its lack of stability: "Mother, monogamy, romance. High spurts in the fountain; fierce and foamy the wild jet. The urge has but a single outlet ... No wonder these pre-moderns were mad and wicked and miserable ... What with mothers and lovers, what with the prohibitions they were not conditioned to obey ... they were forced to feel strongly. And feeling strongly (and strongly, what was more, in solitude, in hopelessly individual isolation), how could they be stable?" And stability is "the primal and ultimate need" of society, the reason for development of the Conditioning Centre.

Essentially, Mond argues that all fierce emotion (painful and pleasurable) chips away at individual (and by extension, societal) stability. These uncontrollable urges are the result of "impulse arrested," which must ultimately spill over, "and the flood is feeling, the flood is passion, the flood is even madness." In order to maintain stability, an individual must have no time to notice unfulfilled desire; by shortening the interval between desire and consummation, the World State is able to maintain a stability that would have been impossible in the old days, which not only permitted passion, but glorified it.

Mond lectures the students (and conveniently, the reader as well) in the birth of the World State, a birth that was not at all peaceful. Originally, the "reformers" were ignored. "Liberalism," "Parliament," and "democracy" (all words with which the students are unfamiliar) banned ectogenesis (literally, "outside birth"), hypnopaedia, and the Caste System. Mond speaks of the Nine Years' War occurring in A. F. 141 (A. D. 2049), which blasted the planet with chemical warfare, anthrax bombs, poisoned water supplies, and thousands of airplane bombers. Following this armageddon was the great Economic Collapse, leading to a final choice between total destruction or World Control, between stability or chaos.

Huxley's descriptions of this future war are clearly informed by the recent (to him) conclusion of World War I. Shocking the world by its violence and destruction, the War was followed by severe economic problems that showed no signs of easing in 1932, when *Brave New World* was published. Huxley's imagined society holds great relevance for his generation, for it is the result of a social and economic situation that surrounded them already.

It took time, however, for the new government to take hold. The original Controllers attempted to change the social fabric by force, beginning with the conscription of consumption. However, this resulted in a "Back to Nature" movement driven by people who refused to purchase and consume the government-mandated amount of goods per year. Mond points out that this "Back to Nature" movement was also "Back to culture. Yes, actually to culture. You can't consume much if you sit still and read books." The initial government response to these "Simple Lifers" was one of force: in the Golders Green Massacre, 800 objectors were killed by machine guns, and in the British Museum Massacre, 2000 were "gassed with dichlorethyl sulphide" (mustard gas, which both Huxley and his original audience had learned to fear during the previous decade's World War I).

Ultimately, the Controllers were forced to turn to less violent means: "The slower but infinitely surer methods of ectogenesis, neo-Pavlovian conditioning and hypnopaedia ... an intensive propaganda campaign against viviparous reproduction ... accompanied by a campaign against the Past; by the closing of museums, the blowing up of historical monuments (luckily most of them had already been destroyed during the Nine Years' War); by the suppression of all books published before A. F. 150 (A. D. 2058)." And the operation was successful; the Controllers were able to condition the population to accept a new world order. The date of Henry Ford's introduction of the T-Model automobile (1908) was chosen as the "opening date of the new era," and "all crosses had their tops cut off and became T's." Instead of "God," the new society celebrates Ford's Day, and sponsors Community Sings, and Solidarity Services. And in place of "Heaven," "the soul," and "immortality," the World State provides soma, a drug that began to be produced commercially in A.F. 178 (A.D. 2086) and provided "all the advantages of Christianity and alcohol; none of their defects." Soma is used every day by the population and is provided by the State; it gives individuals a "holiday from reality," and its constant supply insures stability.

The last hurdle the new State had to overcome was the victory over old age. By developing medical technology that prevented physical and mental maturation beyond a certain point, the State is able to guarantee that "characters remain constant throughout a whole lifetime ... Work, play—at sixty our powers and tastes are what they were at seventeen. Old men in the bad old days used to renounce, retire, take to religion, spend their time reading, thinking—*thinking!*" Now, however, if an individual does find himself with a spare moment, it is always filled with soma.

As Mond finishes his lecture on old age, two children approach him (the tour is still on the playground). The Director shouts angrily at the children, "Go away, little girl! Go away, little boy! Can't you see that his fordship's busy? Go and do you erotic play somewhere else." "His Fordship" Mustapha Mond responds by whispering to himself, "Suffer little children," alluding to the passage from The Gospel of Mark: "And they brought young children to him, that he should touch them: and his disciples rebuked those that brought them. But when Jesus saw it, he was much displeased, and said unto them, Suffer the little children to come unto me, and forbid them not: for of such is the kingdom of God." With this suggestive yet distorted biblical allusion, the chapter, and the tour, concludes. The reader's last impression of Mond recalls the Director's earlier fears that he keeps a secret stash of forbidden books in his office, and hints that perhaps there are cracks in the World State's seemingly flawless map of social stability.

The second storyline (plot 2) begins just after Mustapha Mond joins the student tour. It is four o'clock in the afternoon, time for a shift change at the Conditioning Centre. Henry Foster is in the elevator going up to the Men's Changing Rooms. Henry chats with the Assistant Director of Predestination, both of them pointedly ignoring the third man in the elevator due to his "unsavoury reputation." Henry and the Assistant Director talk about the latest show at the Feelies, Huxley's futuristic version of the cinema, a show that includes tactile and olfactory, as well as visual, stimulation. The Assistant Director asks Henry about Lenina, and Henry answers that "she's a splendid girl. Wonderfully pneumatic. I'm surprised you haven't had her." Henry, who has apparently been "having" Lenina for quite some time, suggests that the Assistant Director "have" her at the first opportunity, repeating what is obviously a hypnopaedic lesson: "Every one belongs to every one else, after all." The men continue their gossip, admiring Lenina's friend Fanny Crowne as very attractive but "not nearly so pneumatic as Lenina." "Pneumatic" seems to be the stock word for female attractiveness, yet another example of how imagery of automation, industry, and of course, anything to do with Henry Ford, permeates this futuristic culture.

During this discussion, the ignored third man in the elevator, Bernard Marx, listens. He is contemptuous of them as they discuss the Feelies, but turns pale when Henry mentions Lenina. In a departure from what Huxley has conditioned the reader to expect from the inhabitants of his world, Bernard is offended on behalf of Lenina: "Talking about her as though she were a bit of meat ... Have her here, have her there. Like mutton. Degrading her to so much mutton." Bernard's sentiments run in opposition to the hypnopaedic lesson recited by Henry; for some reason, he does not seem to instinctively believe that "Every one belongs to every one else." What bothers Bernard most is that Lenina "thinks of herself as meat." In other words, Bernard is upset that Lenina is so normal; for whatever reason, he clearly is not.

Bernard's individuality, coupled with the suggestion of Mond's eccentricities, begins to illuminate a major query of the novel. In this society, which is based wholly upon conformity, what happens to those who are unique? How do they behave toward society? And of course, how does their society deal with them? These questions are more clearly explored later in the novel.

Henry comments on how glum Marx looks, and offers him a gramme of soma. Bernard refuses (thinking how he despises Henry), but Henry insists, backed by the Assistant Director who mockingly recites yet another hypnopaedic lesson: "One cubic centimetre cures ten gloomy sentiments." They persist until Bernard yells at them, cursing, in response to which the two men laugh and exit the elevator. We see Bernard muttering to himself, "Idiots, swine!" subtly echoing Matthew 7:6, "Give not that which is holy unto the dogs, neither cast ye your pearls before swine, lest they trample them under their feet, and turn again and rend you." The implication is that Bernard is in possession of something far more valuable than Foster or the Assistant Director understand. This individuality is something that Bernard must keep secret from those who are "normal," or else that uniqueness will be "trampled" and then the bearer of it, Bernard himself, will be "rent." The allusion in strengthened by its textual proximity to Mustapha Mond's more direct reference to the Bible. This occurs near the end of the chapter, by which point the different plots are textually layered so that the reader, by alternating between them, is essentially reading them simultaneously (which is, of course, how they are happening). Therefore, both Mustapha's and Bernard's surprising (though not necessarily intentional) biblical references occur at the same time, in different locations, and in different plots.

The third plot revolves around Lenina, beginning again at the shift-change. Like Henry, she takes the elevator up to the Girls' Dressing-Room, where she showers and chats with her friend and co-worker, Fanny Crowne (the same Fanny discussed by Henry and the Assistant Director). Although they are not members of a Bokanovsky Group, both girls have the same last name, which is not uncommon as "the two thousand million inhabitants of the planet had only ten thousand names between them." Lenina's shower ritual introduces the reader to several futuristic machines, such as the vibro-vacuum massage machine and the synthetic music machine. These inventions are never fully explained, but they seem to be enhanced versions of what would have been very basic devices during Huxley's lifetime: for example, the synthetic music machine is simply a much-improved radio.

Lenina and Fanny discuss their plans for the evening. To Lenina's surprise, Fanny is not going on a date. She explains (it seems that an evening without a date needs explanation) that she's been feeling unwell and that Dr. Wells prescribed a Pregnancy Substitute. While this is not explained in detail, it seems to be an program of injections of ovarin and placentin, intended to provide a hormonal substitute for pregnancy.

Fanny is appalled that Lenina is planning to go out with Henry Foster that night, noting that Lenina and Henry have been going out regularly for four months. Scandalized that Lenina has not gone out with anyone else during this time, Fanny urges her to see other men as well: "Of course there's no need to give him up. Have somebody else from time to time, that's all. He has other girls, doesn't he? ... Of course he does. Trust Henry Foster to be the perfect gentleman—always correct." Lenina reluctantly agrees, but explains that she "hadn't been feeling very keen on promiscuity lately." Fanny is sympathetic, but reminds her that she must make the effort, as "every one belongs to every one else."

Lenina confides that Bernard Marx invited her to accompany him on a vacation to the Savage Reservation in New Mexico. Fanny is horrified, citing his reputation for spending time alone ("They say he doesn't like Obstacle Golf.") and his less-than-average physical appearance. She gossips: "They say somebody made a mistake when he was still in the bottle—thought he was a Gamma and put alcohol into his blood-surrogate. That's why he's so stunted." Lenina argues that she finds him "rather sweet ... One feels one would like to pet him. You know. Like a cat." This recalls Mond's description of a "mother" as a cat brooding over her kittens; metaphorically, then, Bernard is subtly identified with viviparous existence, rife with passion and exiled from this new society.

Fanny and Lenina's conversation ends with a more light-hearted banter about Lenina's new Malthusian Belt, a gift from Henry Foster. This belt seems to be a stylish vehicle for contraceptives, essential for all females who are not freemartins. Huxley names the belt after Thomas Malthus, a late-eighteenth, early-nineteenth philosopher who observed that nature produces more offspring than can realistically survive. Malthus applied this observation to the human population and argued the necessity the population control as a means to avoid famine and poverty. His ideas were fundamental to Darwin's theory of Natural Selection.

These are the three main plotlines of Chapter Three. As the chapter progresses, the "scenes" get shorter, so that in the last third of the chapter, the scene changes nearly every sentence. At this point, two more scenes are introduced, and are interspersed between the three major plotlines. The first is the hypnopaedic lesson, "Adapting future demand to future industrial supply." I've pieced it together as follows: *I do love flying. I do love flying, I do love having new clothes. But old clothes are beastly. We always throw away old clothes. Ending is better than mending, ending is better than mending, ending is better than mending. The more stitches, the less riches; the more stitches, the less riches.*

The fifth scene appears only once, closing the chapter in the Embryo Store: "Slowly, majestically, with a faint humming of machinery, the Conveyors moved forward, thirty-three centimetres an hour. In the red darkness glinted innumerable rubies."

In part 1 of **chapter 4**, Lenina enters the elevator to leave the building, and recognizes most of the men coming from the Alpha Changing Room. "She was a popular girl and, at one time or another, had spent a night with almost all of them." She spots Bernard huddled in the corner and loudly accepts his invitation to New Mexico. She notices many of her former dates looking shocked that she would associate with someone as disreputable as Marx, but this disapproval spurs her to speak louder ("she was publicly proving her unfaithfulness to Henry. Fanny ought to be pleased, even though it was Bernard.") Bernard is embarrassed by the attention, and blushingly suggests they discuss it elsewhere, when there are fewer people around. Lenina laughs at his eccentricity and the lift arrives at the roof, where its passengers disembark. The sky is humming with helicopters and rocket-planes; air travel seems to be the way of the future. Bernard comments, with a trembling voice, on how beautiful the sky is; Lenina "smiled at him with an expression of the most sympathetic understanding. 'Simply perfect for Obstacle Golf.'" This exchange distills the difference between Bernard and Lenina, or more accurately, the distance between Bernard and the rest of conditioned society. People are not meant to adore beauty for the sake of beauty, but rather see channel everything toward consumerism, like Lenina. Lenina waves goodbye to Bernard and runs across the roof toward Henry's helicopter, anxious that he will be angry if she keeps him waiting.

Benito Hoover, a former date of Lenina's, emerges from the elevator behind Bernard, and comments on how glum he looks. Like Henry in the previous chapter, Benito offers Bernard a gramme of soma, prompting Bernard to rush away.

Lenina reaches Henry's helicopter, where he chastises her for being four minutes late. They lift off and the reader is given an aerial tour of London. We see (with Lenina) the many stadiums and arenas for sports such as Riemann-surface tennis and Escalator Fives. Part One ends as Henry and Lenina land at Stoke Poges and begin to play Obstacle Golf.

Part 2 follows Bernard after Lenina leaves him on the roof. He is very upset: angry at Benito for being so good-natured and at Lenina for being so "normal." He was "wretched that she should have thought it such a perfect afternoon for Obstacle Golf, that she should trotted away to join Henry Foster, that she should have found him funny for not wanting to talk of their most private affairs in public. Wretched, in a word, because she had behaved as any healthy and virtuous English girl ought to behave and not in some other, abnormal, extraordinary way." Bernard is aware that he is not quite "normal"; he is physically well below-average (his "physique was hardly better than that of the average Gamma"), and this physical inferiority "made him feel an outsider; and feeling an outsider he behaved like one, which increased the prejudice against him and intensified the contempt and hostility aroused by his physical defects." He envies men like Henry and Benito who never feel self-conscious about their appearance, men "so utterly at home as to be unaware either of themselves or of the beneficent and comfortable element in which they had their being."

He boards his helicopter and flies to the Bureaux of Propaganda, where he picks up his friend Helmholtz Watson. Helmholtz works as a lecturer at the College of Emotional Engineering, and as a writer for *The Hourly Radio* (an upper-caste newspaper); he also composes Feely scripts and hypnopaedic rhymes. Unlike Bernard, Helmholtz is physically perfect. However, he feels smarter than everyone else, making him an outsider like Bernard: "What the two men shared was the knowledge that they were individuals."

Helmholtz accompanies Bernard to his apartment, where he speaks of a strange urge that he has been unable to identify. The reader easily recognizes this urge as the desire to exert his individuality; Helmholtz is unable to name it, for no matter how intelligent, he is still a conditioned member of society. He asks Bernard, "Did you ever feel as though you had something inside you that was only waiting for you to give it a chance to come out? Some sort of extra power that you aren't using—you know, like all the water that goes down the falls instead of through the turbines?" The image if controlled water echoes Mond's description of emotion in chapter 3 as water spurting roughly from a single puncture in a pipe.

Bernard interrupts Helmholtz, thinking he hears someone at the door. This sort of conversation is forbidden, and so the nervous Bernard checks to make sure they are truly alone. They are, and Bernard is embarrassed at his nerves. He complains to Helmholtz, excusing his behavior by bewailing how suspicious people are of him, and how much that makes him suspicious of everyone else. Helmholtz listens, but feels a bit ashamed for his friend. "He wished Bernard would show a little more pride."

Huxley takes us back to Stoke Poges in part 1 of **chapter 5**, now eight o'clock and post sunset. Lenina and Henry board his helicopter and fly back to London, passing over the monorail trains that provide transportation for the lower castes (who presumably cannot afford their own helicopters). They pass the Slough Crematorium, where smokestacks release the chemicals of each human body as it is burned. Not only does the crematorium produce jobs and necessitate industry (as opposed to the materials and labor required by a graveyard), but it also incorporates a phosphorous recovery program, in which 98% of the phosphorous emitted from a burning human body is recovered, totaling four hundred tons of phosphorous from England each year. Henry perfectly sums up his society's attitude: "Fine to think we can go being socially useful even after we're dead. Making plants grow."

Lenina has a slightly more creative reaction; she adds: "But queer that Alphas and Betas won't make any more plants grow than those nasty little Gammas and Deltas and Epsilons ..." Henry answers with a stock response, sounding suspiciously like a hypnopaedic lesson: "All men are physico-chemically equal ... Besides, even Epsilons perform indispensable services." One should not ignore the similarity of Henry's statement to the post-Enlightenment sentiment, "All men are created equal." For this, of course, is no longer true in Huxley's world. As they leave the Crematorium behind, neither Henry nor Lenina are disturbed by the thought of death; as Henry repeats, "there's one thing we can be certain of; whoever he may have been, he was happy when he was alive. Everybody's happy now."

Back at Henry's apartment, the couple eats dinner and takes soma with coffee after the meal. They go to the Westminster Abbey Cabaret (Huxley's cathedral ironically transformed into a cabaret) to see the latest Synthetic Music show. All doped up on soma, hundreds of couples dance suggestively to the music; Huxley's language associates the dancing with sexual intercourse, and the music with arousal culminating in orgasm. The "musicians," Calvin Stopes and His Sixteen Sexophonists, conclude the show with a song beginning, "Bottle of mine." Unlike twentieth-century songs beginning with similar lyrics, however, the bottle to which they refer is filled not with beer or whiskey, but peritoneum lining, blood-surrogate, and carefully-engineered embryos.

Henry and Lenina, due to the combination of soma and music, are swept away in the entertainment (they are on a soma-holiday), and "bottled" (drunk), they return to Henry's apartment. As they climb into bed, Lenina, as though by instinct (or conditioning) remembers to take her contraceptives to avoid a viviparous situation.

After dining with Helmholtz, Bernard flies to the Fordson Community Singery for his biweekly Solidarity Service in part 2. He arrives just as Big Henry (as opposed to Big Ben) strikes nine o'clock: he is late. He arrives at Room 3210 (countdown?) just in time, pleased that he is not the last to arrive. Bernard sits next to Morgana Rothschild, and is embarrassed when he must admit to her that he did not spend the afternoon playing Obstacle or Electromagnetic Golf. As the service begins, Bernard is pessimistic about its outcome; he "foresaw for himself yet another failure to achieve atonement." The Solidarity Service, then, seems to be Huxley's answer to going to church. The Service progresses as follows:

The twelve members of the group (reminiscent of the Twelve Apostles) sit in a circle, alternating males and females. The President of the Group stands, makes the sign of the "T," and switches on the synthetic music. A cup of strawberry ice-cream soma is passed between the twelve, each drinking after reciting, "I drink to my annihilation." Three Solidarity Hymns are sung, interspersed with other liturgical recitations: "I drink to the Greater Being," and "I drink to the imminence of His Coming." Each hymn focuses on the coming of the "Greater Being" and the simultaneous merging of individual existence into this Greater Being. Unlike Christian regenerative theology, which begs salvation of the individual through God, Huxley's "religion" seems to call for the annihilation of the individual and the subsequent *creation* of a God, the Greater Being or Twelve-in-One. The supreme deity in Bernard's society is not a larger-than-life individual, but the aggregate of all human individuals in one mass being.

After the singing of the hymns, the Solidarity Group engages in a sort of pentecostal frenzy, the synthetic voice instructing them to listen for the feet of the Greater Being. Soon, one of the members (Morgana) jumps up, claiming to hear him, prompting the others to follow suit. Bernard, "feeling that it was time for him to do something ... also jumped up and shouted, 'I hear him; He's coming,' But it wasn't true. He heard nothing and, for him, nobody was coming." As usual, Bernard is different from his peers; what makes him different is his awareness of his own individuality. He is unable to annihilate himself for the coming of the Twelve-in-One.

The Group dances in circles, becoming more frenetic and now singing "Orgy-porgy," the lyrics of which recall sexual imagery, much as did the music at the Westminster Abbey Cabaret. The lights dim until "they were dancing in the crimson twilight of the Embryo Store," and the service culminates in what appears to be an orgy.

After the service, Fifi Bradlaugh, another member of Bernard's Solidarity Group, approaches him and comments on how wonderful the service was. He agrees with her, but is lying; he feels: "separate and unatoned, while the others were being fused into the Greater Being ... the sight of [Fifi's] transfigured face was at once an accusation and an ironical reminder of his own separateness. He was as miserably isolated now as he had been when the service began—more isolated by reason of his unreplenished emptiness, his dead satiety."

In **chapter 6**, part 1, several weeks have passed, and Lenina questions her decision to accompany Bernard to New Mexico. She has gone on several dates with him and finds him increasingly strange. Her other option, however, is returning to the North Pole with George Edzel, which she found quite boring last summer. She is ultimately enticed by the opportunity to visit a Savage Reservation, which requires a special permit (Bernard has one) and is quite a rare occurrence (only six people in the entire Conditioning Centre had ever visited one). She confides her worries about Bernard to Fanny, who again claims that his oddness is due to alcohol in his blood-surrogate. Henry, however, refers to Bernard as a "rhinoceros," explaining that some men simply "don't respond properly to conditioning."

Lenina remembers her first date with Bernard: nixing her suggestion of Electro-Magnetic Golf, Bernard proposes that they go for a long walk, where they can be alone and talk. Lenina is shocked by the suggestion, and finally persuades him to fly to Amsterdam and attend the Semi-Demi Finals of the Women's Heavyweight Wrestling Competition. Bernard, of course, has a miserable time. He becomes more and more frustrated with Lenina, who responds to his unhappiness with a number of hypnopaedic rhymes. She tempts him with soma in order to cure his bad mood with the lure, "A gramme is always better than a damn." But Bernard still refuses, arguing, "I'd rather be myself ... Myself and nasty. Not somebody else, however jolly."

On this flight back to London, Bernard cuts the engines and hovers the helicopter low above the storming waters of the English Channel, ordering Lenina to look down. She is terrified of the darkness and the silence, and urges Bernard to continue flying. He tries to make her understand why he loves looking into the dark water: "It makes me feel as though ... as though I were more *me*, if you see what I mean. More on my own, not so completely a part of something else. Not just a cell in the social body." Lenina becomes more and more upset, refusing to listen to Bernard as he goes on to talk of his desire to be "free" from his conditioning. Finally, Bernard submits to Lenina's tears, obviously disappointed in her inability to try to understand his thoughts. They return to his rooms, where Bernard takes a large dose of soma, and they go to bed.

The next afternoon, Lenina asks Bernard if he enjoyed himself the night before, and is unsettled and confused when he tells her that he wishes they had not slept together on their first date. Again, she cannot understand his reasons, and assumes that he means that she was not attractive enough. He explains that he would have like to try "the effect of arresting

[his] impulses," but once more Lenina responds with a hypnopaedic lesson: "Never put off till to-morrow the fun you can have today."

The chapter concludes with Lenina confiding her anxieties to Fanny, but still insisting: "All the same ... I do like him. He has such awfully nice hands. And the way he moves his shoulders—that's very attractive ... But I wish he weren't so odd."

In final preparations for his trip to the Savage Reservation, Bernard visits the Director's office to get his signature on the permit in part 2. The Director surprises Bernard by recounting his own visit, years ago, to the New Mexican reservation. Like Bernard, he took a girl there on vacation, but during the night she wandered off and was lost in a huge thunderstorm. The Director himself lost the horses and had to crawl back to the rest-house. Although a massive search was conducted, the girl (a Beta-Minus) could not be found, and it was concluded that she came upon some mishap in the desert and was killed. The Director tells Bernard how frightening the whole ordeal was, and how long he was plagued my nightmares of thunderstorms and the wilderness.

As abruptly as the Director began his tale, he concludes it, embarrassed and angry that he revealed such a "discreditable secret." To cover for his lapse in judgment (and, as he sees it, a revelation of weakness), the Director berates Bernard for his less-than-normal extracurricular activities (that is, his *lack* of activities). He explains that it is Bernard's duty to conform: "Alphas are conditioned that they do not *have* to be infantile in their emotional behaviour. But that is all the more reason for their making a special effort to conform. It is their duty to be infantile, even against their inclination." He completes his lecture by warning Bernard that unless he makes a better effort to conform to societal standards, he will face exile to a Sub-Centre, possible the one in Iceland.

Bernard leaves the office exalted, feeling as though he emerged from an adventure as the hero. Of course, he is certain that the Director's threats will never actually occur; as such, he is able to revel in his "rebellion" without actually facing any consequences. That evening, Bernard exaggerates the encounter to Helmholtz, who sees his friend's hypocrisy and boasting. As in the previous chapter, Helmholtz is ashamed for Bernard, and wishes he were less boastful and self-pitying.

A week later, Bernard and Lenina take the Blue Pacific Rocket to Santa Fé in part 3. They spend the night there, and meet with the Warden of the Reservation the following morning. He lectures them on the specifics of the reservation: it covers 560,000 square kilometers and is divided into four Sub-Reservations, each contained by an electric fence that prevents escape (it kills on contact). The reservation contains approximately 60,000 Indians (although it is impossible to keep an accurate count), and preserves viviparous life: marriage, families, religion, extinct languages, infectious disease, ferocious animals, priests. After outlining the makeup of the reservation, the Warden signs their permit and arranges for a Reservation Guard to fly them into the reservation.

While they wait, Bernard telephones Helmholtz because he fears he left a cologne-tap running in his apartment. Helmholtz informs him that the Director announced that he was looking for a replacement for Bernard in the Conditioning Centre, hinting that Bernard would be exiled to Iceland. Bernard is terribly upset (not at all like to isolated hero of the previous week when Iceland was just a distant threat), and is anxious to conform if the Director would only give him another opportunity: "He raged against himself—what a fool!—against the Director—how unfair not to give him another chance, that other chance which, he now had no doubt at all, he had always intended to take." This summarizes that hypocrisy that Helmholtz sees in Bernard; as soon as he is actually faced with being an individual, he wishes nothing other than a chance to act as conditioned as Lenina.

Lenina persuades Bernard to take soma, and they board the plane that flies them over the Reservation. Bernard sleeps, and wakes only when they land in Malpais, their destination for the afternoon and where they will spend the night. The chapter ends as the helicopter lifts off, leaving them with an Indian guide, but not before the pilot reminds them: "They're perfectly tame;

savages won't do you any harm. They've got enough experience of gas bombs to know that they mustn't play any tricks."

In **chapter 7**, Bernard and Lenina climb the mesa to Malpais, following an Indian guide whom, Lenina distastefully notices, stinks. Huxley notes that the pueblo looks like a collection of "amputated pyramids," recalling Mond's lecture to the students in which he describes "some things called the pyramids," that were destroyed in the "campaign against the past." Lenina likens this alien world to London: the mesa is "like the Charing-T Tower," and the naked Indians, painted with white lines, remind her of "asphalt tennis courts." She and Bernard are shocked when they witness old age, a phenomenon that has been eradicated from their society. Lenina sees a mother nursing her child, and reaches desperately for her soma, only to discover that she left it at the rest-house. Presumably for the first time in her life, Lenina must face unpleasantness without soma. The two are led to a terrace from which they can look down into the village square where a ritual is about to begin. Lenina is comforted by the steady banging of drums, reminding "her reassuringly of the synthetic noises made at Solidarity Services and Ford's Day celebrations." This comfort is short-lived; the ritual is one of pain and blood, and Lenina becomes more and more distraught at the sight of a young man being whipped until he faints.

As the ritual ends, Lenina sits in shock covering her face with her hands. Bernard turns as a young Indian enters the room, and he is surprised that this Indian, in addition to being blond-haired and blue-eyed, can speak flawless English. The savage, John, is thrilled to meet "civilized" people; he explains that he is the son of a woman who visited the Reservation years ago. Apparently, his mother had fallen while taking a walk, and the Indians had brought her to the pueblo to care for her. Her escort, a man named Tomakin, "must have flown away, back to the Other Place, away without her—a bad, unkind, unnatural man." Bernard immediately realizes that this young man must be the son of the Director (whose first name is Thomas, surprisingly similar to "Tomakin"), and his mother the Beta-Minus woman he assumed dead.

John calls his mother, Linda, into the room. Smelling of alcohol (as Lenina observes, she "simply reeked of that beastly stuff that was put into Delta and Epsilon bottles"), grossly overweight, and incredibly dirty, Linda is hysterical at the sight of "civilized" people. She rushes at Lenina and hugs her, nearly making her sick. Bernard and John take a walk outside of the house, leaving Linda to fawn over Lenina's silk-acetate clothing and Malthusian belt. She tells Lenina that she found herself to be pregnant after her fall and rescue by the Indians; apparently the Malthusian contraceptives sometimes fail to work, but in the Reservation there are no Abortion Centres, so Linda was forced to give birth. She tried as best she could to "condition" John, teaching him what hypnopaedic rhymes she remembered as nursery rhymes, attempting to protect him from the insanity of the savages. Linda laments the lack of soma in the Reservation; once reliant on the drug, she had turned to the nearest thing she can find: mescal. While soma is not physically addictive, mescal is, and Linda has become an alcoholic.

The Indians saw Linda as a prostitute, as she could not understand the savage belief in monogamy. In addition to her white skin and strange ways, this turned her and John into something like outcasts. John, for instance, desperately wanted to participate in the coming-of-age ritual witnessed earlier, but is excluded because of his "complexion." He claims that he would have been a much stronger participant than the boy they chose (the boy who was beaten until unconscious); he says: "They could have had twice as much blood from me. The multitudinous seas incarnadine ... But they wouldn't let me. They disliked me for my complexion. It's always been like that. Always." John's reference to Shakespeare is surprising: he alludes to Macbeth's speech in Act II: "Will all great Neptune's ocean wash this blood / Clean from my hand? No, this my hand will rather / The multitudinous seas incarnadine, / Making the green one red." John, half-conditioned, half-savage, somehow knows Macbeth well enough to quote it.

The Chapter closes with Linda bewailing her condition, specifically, her inability to completely civilize her son. Particularly in regard to sexual relations, John's beliefs are those of the Indians, rather than those of his mother. Linda tells Lenina: "Once ... he tried to kill poor Waihusiwa—or was it Popé?—just because I used to have them sometimes. Because I never *could* make him understand that that was what civilized people ought to do. Being mad's infectious, I believe." With this last potentially prophetic statement, the chapter ends.

While Linda bewails her condition to Lenina, Bernard and John speak outside of the building in **chapter 8**. Bernard is curious about John's life, and begs him to tell his story "from the beginning. As far back as you can remember." What follows is John's first-person narrative of his history, composed of anecdotes and incidents, sometimes with years in between. These memories will be divided into episodes for easier reference.

Episode 1: John is quite young, and remembers Linda singing him her version of lullabies to help him fall asleep. Not knowing any traditional lullabies, she sings whatever rhymes she can recall from the "Other Place": "Streptocock-Gee to Banbury-T" and "Bye Baby Banting, soon you'll need decanting." John falls asleep, but is awakened by laughing. He sees an Indian man with hair "like two black ropes" in bed with Linda, whispering to her and making her laugh. Frightened, John snuggles against Linda, prompting her to tell the man, "Not with John here." Rather than leaving, however, the man pulls John out of the bed and locks him in a back room. John yells for his mother, but she neither answers nor frees him; she is presumably engaged sexually with the Indian.

Episode 2: Still a child, John plays with Indian boys in the weaving room, while their mothers work the looms. Suddenly, Linda gets into an argument with an Indian woman and is pushed out of the room; John follows her and discovers that she broke something. She says, "How should I know how to do their beastly weaving? Beastly savages." Popé waits for them at their house, and he gives Linda a gourd of mescal, which she quickly drinks and passes out in bed.

Episode 3: John recalls an afternoon he returned to their house to find several Indian women beating Linda. Screaming, he tries to intervene, only to be knocked to the ground and whipped several times himself. That evening, he asks Linda why the women wanted to hurt her. She tells him that she does not really understand, but that the women said "those men are *their* men"; Linda is being punished for her promiscuity, conditioned as "normal" behavior since she was an infant. John tries to hug his mother, but she is repulsed by her "son," and beats him out of her frustration, screaming, "Turned into a savage. Having young ones like an animal ... If it hadn't been for you, I might have gone to the Inspector, I might have got away. But not with a baby. That would have been too shameful." Linda finally stops hitting John, suddenly hugging and kissing him. This incident, in addition to John's others stories about Linda, illustrates how she is split between her instinct to mother her son and her conditioning to hate all things viviparous. Her conditioning does not seem to have completely wiped out her natural instinct, but it has affected her so that she can never completely love her son.

Episode Four: John's favorite childhood memories are of Linda's stories about the Other Place, or the "civilized" world. He is enchanted by her tales of elaborate games and Feelies, electric lighting and Scent Organs, "and people never lonely, but living together and being so jolly and happy, like the summer dances here is Malpais, but much happier, and the happiness being there every day ..." Linda's stories are contrasted by the tales of one of the elders in the pueblo, who speaks to the children about the mystical religion of the Indians, which seems to be a fusion of Christianity and nature worship. The two different mythologies combine in John's head: "Lying in bed, he would think of Heaven and London and Our Lady of Acoma and the rows and rows of babies in clean bottles and Jesus flying up and Linda flying up and the great Director of the World hatcheries and Awonawilona."

Episode Five: Linda continues to see many different men, prompting the pueblo to label her a whore. Even the children mocked her, a song of theirs inciting John to throw stones at them. The stone-throwing fight is weighted in favor of the Indian boys, and ends with John covered in blood.

Episode Six: Writing simple rhymes on the wall with charcoal, Linda teaches John to read. Once he learns the basics, she gives him the book she had the day she was lost: *The Chemical and Bacteriological Conditioning of the Embryo. Practical Instructions for Beta Embryo-Store Workers.* John is frustrated and bored with the book, but begins to see his ability to read as a sort of revenge against the Indian boys who continually mock his mother. Her book raises a number of questions for him, questions that Linda, with her limited and very specific training, is unable to answer. Her explanation for the existence of things is always practical, but of no use in the pueblo. For example, she explains that "chemicals" come from bottles that come from the Chemical Store. John is much more intrigued by the Indian explanation for existence: "The seed of men and all creatures, the seed of the sun and the seen of the earth and the seed of the sky—Awonawilona made them all out of the Fog of Increase." Again, John is trained by two opposing worlds, making his viewpoint unique and not entirely acceptable by either society.

Episode Seven: Soon after his twelfth birthday, Linda gives John an old book that Popé found in an ancient chest. Linda supposes the book to be "uncivilized," but thinks it must be useful for John to practice his reading. The book is called *The Complete Works of William Shakespeare*. John opens the book at random, and the first passage he reads is from the third act of *Hamlet*, with Hamlet berating his mother for her infidelity: "Nay, but to live / In the rank sweat of an enseamed bed, / Stew'd in corruption, honeying and making love / Over thy nasty sty...." The passage affects John "like the drums at the summer dances, if the drums could have spoken." He feels that it speaks directly to him and his situation, "about Linda lying there snoring, with the empty cup on the floor beside the bed; about Linda and Popé...."

Episode Eight: As John reads Shakespeare, he begins to hate Popé more and more, associating him with such Shakespearean villains as Iago and, above all, Claudius. He sees Shakespeare's words as magic, "and somehow it was as though he had never really hated Popé before; never really hated him because he had never been able to say how much he hated him." Literature is here endowed with the power to *create* emotion—John's reaction to Shakespeare is the perfect example of why literature is banned in London. When he reads of Hamlet's desire to murder Claudius, "when he is drunk asleep, or in his rage / Or in the incestuous pleasure of his bed," John is convinced that the words are telling him to kill Popé. He stabs Popé, who is lying "drunk asleep" in Linda's bed, but misses his mark and merely wounds him. Rather than beating John, however, Popé laughs at his tears, and sends him out of the room, calling him "my brave Ahaiyuta."

Episode Nine: John is fifteen, and Mitsima, an elder Indian, takes him to the river and teaches him how to work the clay into a traditional Indian pot. John's pot is messy and unusable, but he is incredibly happy to be included, even by one old man, in Indian tradition and education.

Episode Ten: John, now sixteen, waits outside of a house while a marriage ceremony takes place within. The bride and groom emerge and perform traditional Indian rituals, conducted by Mitsima. Linda scoffs at the ceremony, thinking that "it does seem a lot of fuss to make about so little." John, however, is profoundly affected, and runs away from the crowd. He is heartbroken, for he is in love with the bride, Kiakimé. Of course, John is unable to speak of this to Linda, as it is yet another example of his "savagery," or her failure to properly condition him.

Episode Eleven: It is a special evening in the pueblo, for it is the night in which the young men perform the rituals that announce their manhood. Excited and nervous, John follows the Indian teens to the ladder leading into the Antelope Kiva, an underground cave in which the ritual takes place. Yet as he prepares to follow the others down into the Kiva, he is stopped and struck by the observers, who yell, "Not for you, white-hair! Not for the son of the she-dog!" Amidst a shower of stones, John runs out onto the mesa, where he stares off the edge of the precipice, contemplating suicide. He sees blood drip from a wound on his hand, and thinks of *Macbeth*: "To-morrow and to-morrow and to-morrow ... [John] had discovered Time and

Death and God." In other words, his solitude and learning eventually introduced John to the three things most feared by "civilized" society, foreshadowing his inability to exist in that world any better that he exists in the world of the Indians.

Bernard is struck by John's description of his loneliness, and relates to him as an outsider in his society. John is surprised, citing Linda's descriptions of London, which revolve around the idea that no one is ever alone. Bernard blushingly explains, "I'm rather different from most people, I suppose. If one happens to be decanted different...." John is quick to understand: "If one's different, one's bound to be lonely."

Bernard invites John and Linda to return to London with him and Lenina, "making the first move in a campaign whose strategy he had been secretly elaborating ever since, in the little house, he had realized who the "father" of this young savage must be." Recall that John's father is the Director, the man planning to exile Bernard to Iceland. If Bernard can embarrass him by presenting his viviparous "son," then presumably he will gain the leverage needed to negotiate his position and remain in London. John, however, is unaware of this ulterior motive, and is thrilled by the prospect of finally seeing the Other Place. He quotes Miranda from *The Tempest*, when she finally gets the opportunity to see mankind outside of her father on their small island: "O wonder! ... How many goodly creatures are there here! How beauteous mankind is! ... O brave new world that has such people in it." Bernard is perplexed by John's Shakespearean language, and the chapter ends with his reaction to the passage: "Hadn't you better wait till you actually see the new world?"

In **chapter 9**, Lenina returns to the hotel in Malpais after her "day of queerness and horror"; she treats herself to a dose of soma large enough to give her an eighteen-hour holiday. Bernard, on the other hand, lies awake all night perfecting his plan to bring John and Linda back to London. In the morning, while Lenina is still "on *soma*-holiday," he flies to Santa Fé and calls the World Controller's Office in London. After telling his story to several undersecretaries, Bernard is connected directly to Mustapha Mond, who asks Bernard to bring the two "savages" back as a matter of scientific interest. Feeling very important after speaking with a World Controller, Bernard obtains the necessary passes from the Warden and returns to Malpais before Lenina wakes up.

While Bernard is in Santa Fé, John approaches the hotel where Lenina and Bernard are staying. He was invited to visit them, but receives no answer when he knocks at the door. Terrified that the two foreigners left without him (and upset because he thinks he will never again have the chance to see Lenina, on whom he has developed a substantial infatuation), John smashes a window and crawls into Lenina's room. He sees her luggage and is relieved to know that she has not yet left; he assumes that she is simply out of the hotel. He furtively rifles through her suitcase, delighting in civilized accoutrements such as her perfumed handkerchiefs, scented powder, and zippicamiknicks (apparently her undergarment). He is startled to hear a noise coming from the bedroom, and he hastily stuffs her possessions back in the suitcase and sneaks over to investigate the source of the noise. He finds Lenina, lying semiconscious on soma-holiday in her bed, wearing pink zippyjamas. John nearly cries with her beauty, and is inspired to recited a passage from Shakespeare's *Troilus and Cressida*, in which Troilus obsesses over the seemingly supernatural whiteness of Cressida's hand; the passage reminds him of another Shakespearean passage, and he continues, whispering Romeo's adulation of Juliet's hand. Both passages concern the extreme purity of the heroine. By piling the significance of whiteness—virginity, purity, chastity—onto Lenina, John creates an image of her as the embodiment of all these things. Lenina, however, is neither virginal nor chaste, which has the potential to cause much friction between John's expectations of Lenina and Lenina herself.

John is interrupted by the sound of buzzing; the helicopter carrying Bernard is landing outside. He just has time to run from the room and through the open window before he meets Bernard, who is of course expecting him.

The narrative returns to London in **chapter 10**. In the Hatchery and Conditioning Centre, the Director and Henry

Foster walk into the Fertilizing Room, where the Director has asked Bernard to meet hem. He plans to publicly announce Bernard's exile, making an example of him. Henry points out that for all of his eccentricities, Bernard still does his work quite well, prompting the Director to launch into a series of hypnopaedic axioms such as, "His intellectual eminence carries with it corresponding moral responsibilities," and "The greater a man's talents, the greater his power to lead astray." Therefore although Bernard is a valuable worker, "unorthodoxy threatens more than the life of a mere individual; it strikes at Society itself," and "it is better that one should suffer than that many should be corrupted."

Bernard enters, and the Director asks for the attention of all the workers in the room, and describes Bernard's flaws, from his heretical views on soma to the abnormality of his sex life. He concludes his harangue by sentencing Bernard to exile in Iceland, where he will be unable to corrupt innocent workers. More as a formality than anything else, the Director asks Bernard if he has anything to say in his defense. Bernard surprises him by bringing in Linda, who quite obscenely runs up to "her Tomakin," the Director, and hugs him desperately. Her appearance shocks everyone in the room; no one is accustomed or prepared to see the signs of old age and malnutrition. The Director is shocked, but the situation worsens exponentially when she reveals that she bore him a son after she was lost. John then enters, approaches the Director, kneels before him, and says, "My father!" Unlike the word "mother," which implies gross incorrectness and made the observers feel extremely uncomfortable, "father" is "a scatological rather than a pornographic impropriety." Gasps turn to hysterical laughter, and the Director flees the room in disgrace.

In **chapter 11**, Bernard's revelation of John and Linda causes a sensation in London. The Director resigns in humiliation, and John becomes a cross between a celebrity and novelty act. All of uppercaste London clamors to meet him, and his notoriety spills over to his guardian and chaperone, Bernard. Bernard no longer has difficulty convincing women to go out with him (a fact about which he brags to Helmholtz, causing a rift between them when Bernard accuses Helmholtz of jealousy), and his parties becomes the hottest ticket in town, for it is only through Bernard that one is able to meet "the savage."

London is less amused by Linda, a failure of conditioning rather than a true savage. Her grotesque appearance makes conditioned citizens physically ill. Furthermore, her being a "mother" is simply obscene, while John's "sonhood" is an interesting and forgivable (to an extent) eccentricity. Linda is not bothered by her ostracization, as she is thrilled with the newly-available supply of soma. Greedy for endless holiday, she lies in a bedroom 24 hours a day, constantly taking higher doses of soma. Dr. Shaw admits that, at this rate of consumption, the soma will kill Linda in a matter of months. No one but John, however, see this as a problem, and even John is convinced that Linda will be happier living two months on bliss than years in unhappiness. Dr. Shaw explains that in a way, soma will actually *lengthen* Linda's life: "Every *soma*-holiday is a bit of what our ancestors used to call eternity."

Bernard escorts John around London, touring everything from the Weather Department's balloon in the sky to the Electrical Equipment Corporation to Eton, the futuristic incarnation of England's prestigious boarding school. John is less than impressed. He finds the immense speed of the Bombay Green Rocket sub-par in comparison to Shakespeare's Ariel, who "could put a girdle round the earth in forty minutes." Seeing masses of Bokanovsky Groups make him physically sick, and he again recalls *The Tempest*, this time ironically remembering Miranda's excitement, "O brave new world that has such people in it." John's lack of excitement prompts Bernard to send a concerned letter to Mustapha Mond, in which he timidly admits to agreeing with some of John's ideas: "I must admit that I agree with the Savage in finding civilized infantility too easy or, as he put it, not expensive enough; and I would like to take this opportunity of drawing your fordship's attention to...." Bernard's self-importance evokes laughter from Mond, who thinks that one day he will have to teach Bernard a lesson about the social order.

Lenina too has become a bit of a celebrity due to her association with "the savage." She has been on dates with men as important as the Resident World Controller's Second Secretary and the Arch-Community-Songster of Canterbury. She confides to Fanny that much of the attention is due to the assumption that she has made love to John, which much to her disappointment and confusion, she has not. She is very attracted to him, and often catches him staring at her, but he seems reluctant to admit that he finds her desirable.

The last part of the chapter follows Lenina on an evening with John (Bernard is going out on a date himself, and asks Lenina to escort John to the Feelies). They go to see a Feely titled, "Three Weeks in a Helicopter. An All-Super-Singing, Synthetic-Talking, Coloured, Stereoscopic Feely with Synchronized Scent-Organ Accompaniment." The story is that of a black man whose conditioning is wiped from his brain after a helicopter accident. He falls madly in love with a Beta-Plus blonde, kidnaps her, and holds her captive in his helicopter for three weeks. She is rescued finally by three men, who send the man off to an Adult Re-Conditioning Centre (apparently this new society is prepared for incidents in which conditioning fails) and take the blonde as a mistress. Thus it ends conventionally. John is aroused by the show, and desperately desires Lenina, who obviously expects him to stay the night in her apartment. He is ashamed of his desire, and refuses to look too long at Lenina, "obscurely terrified lest she should cease to be something he could feel himself worthy of ... 'I don't think you ought to see things like that,' he said, making haste to transfer from Lenina herself to the surrounding circumstances the blame for any past or possible future lapse from perfection." Lenina is confused by John's condemnation of what she thought was a "lovely" film. She attempts to convince him to come in to her apartment when the taxicopter arrives, but he quickly tells her goodnight and flies away. He hurries home where he desperately re-reads *Othello*, comparing the plot to that of "Three Weeks in a Helicopter." Lenina copes with her disappointment by taking an extra half-gramme of soma.

Bernard is having another of his parties in **chapter 12**, this one particularly prestigious because the Arch-Community-Songster of Canterbury has accepted the invitation. John yells at Bernard for not asking whether or not he wanted to have another party in his honor, and refuses to leave his locked room. Instead, he sits in solitude and reads *Romeo and Juliet*.

Bernard pleads with John to leave his bedroom and come down to the party, but John has lost interest in being a novelty. Humiliated, Bernard announces that the guest of honor will not appear. His guest are quite angry, abandoning their politeness toward Bernard, "furious at having been tricked into behaving politely to this insignificant fellow with the unsavoury reputation and the heretical opinions." Bernard's short-lived celebrity is over.

Lenina accompanied the Arch-Songster to the party, and is particularly upset at John's absence. Still confused about his actions during their evening at the Feelies, she had decided to confess to him that she liked him more than she had ever liked another man. She assumes that his refusal to appear is because he does not like her and does not want to see her. She "felt all the sensations normally experienced at the beginning of a Violent Passion Surrogate treatment—a sense of dreadful emptiness, a breathless apprehension, a nausea. Her heart seemed to stop beating." Against all of her conditioning, Lenina seems to be experiencing emotion. Like Bernard and Helmholtz Watson, she is treading the line between behavior that is acceptable to conditioned society, and that which is strictly forbidden.

The narrative skips to the office of Mustapha Mond, who reads a paper titled, "A New Theory of Biology." Mond acts as censor, reading new material such as this paper, and then deciding whether it is suitable for publication. He deems this paper "*Not to be published*," reflecting that "it was a masterly piece of work. But once you began admitting explanations in terms of purpose—well, you didn't know what the result might be." Mond worries that this paper, and others like it, has the potential to upset some of the "more unsettled minds" in London's uppercaste, and spark ideas that "the purpose of life was not the maintenance of well-being, but some enlargement of knowledge. Which was, the Controller reflected, quite possibly true. But not, in the present circumstances, admissible." While John's appearance in London seems to be bringing out heretical elements in good citizens like Lenina, "uncivilized" elements already exist in the society, and they exist in the minds of the most powerful. Some people, such as Mond, realize that conditioning is not a moral decision, but a practical one, and that it does come with a price—new ideas and progress.

Huxley takes us back to Bernard's room, where he weeps in his humiliation after all of his guests leave. Unlike the Bernard from the first half of the novel, he copes with his despair by taking soma and going to sleep. The following day, he gets sympathy from both John and Helmholtz, who forgives him for abandoning their friendship during his brief celebrity. Bernard, however, is both grateful to and resentful of both men, and is overwhelmingly jealous that the two of them immediately become friends. Helmholtz has recently been in a bit of trouble with "Authority" as the result of reading to his students a rhyme he had written about the joys of solitude. He reads the poem to John, who in turn pulls out his copy of *The Complete Works of William Shakespeare* and reads to Helmholtz. The two men begin to meet regularly, delighting in finding another who appreciates the lyrics of Shakespeare. They are always accompanied by Bernard, who does not understand their fascination with the forbidden author and takes every opportunity to interrupt the recitations and make fun of them.

Helmholtz loves listening to Shakespeare's words, and the reader is reminded of his earlier feeling that he could write something more meaningful if only he had something to write about. Shakespeare's plots, while sometimes a bit "ridiculous" and "mad," show Helmholtz the sorts of situations that inspire meaningful composition. When John begins reading *Romeo and Juliet*, however, Helmholtz is unable to step outside of his conditioning enough to become engrossed in the play. He laughs hysterically when Juliet threatens suicide if she is forced to marry Paris; he cannot understand the concept of monogamous love. John is offended by Helmholtz's disrespect for the story, for he sees it as an analog for his relationship with Lenina. He locks the book back up in its drawer, "with the gesture of one who removes his pearl from before swine." Helmholtz apologizes, explaining, "You can't expect me to keep a straight face about fathers and mothers. And who's going to get excited about a boy having a girl or not having her?" Helmholtz reads Shakespeare as an outline—a method of teaching himself how to compose something meaningful. He is disappointed in *Romeo and Juliet* because it is too unrealistic for him: "No ... it won't do. We need some other kind of madness and violence."

In **chapter 13**, Lenina is at work in the Embryo Store when Henry Foster asks her to accompany him to a Feely. She declines, and Henry notes "weariness," "pallor," and "sadness" in her face. "Afraid that she might be suffering from one of the few remaining infectious diseases," he suggests she visit a doctor and have a Pregnancy Substitute or a Violent Passion Surrogate (V.P.S.). Lenina is irritated by this last suggestion: "She would have laughed, if she hadn't been on the point of crying. As though she hadn't got enough V. P. of her own." Thinking of John, she is so distracted that she loses track of which bottles she has already immunized with a sleeping sickness vaccination. This utopian, perfectly immunized society is still subject to human error, and Lenina's mistake will cause a young Alpha-Minus to die of the disease, "the first case for over half a century."

Fanny is shocked by Lenina's unhealthy obsession with a single man. She first attempts to convince Lenina that there is no reason to focus on only one man (recall her conversation with Lenina in Chapter Three regarding Lenina's potential monogamy with Henry). When Lenina insists that she can't stop thinking of John, Fanny changes tactics, seeing Lenina's obsession as the result of John's refusal to "be had." She tells Lenina to simply "go and take him ... whether he wants it or no."

Inspired by Fanny's firmness, Lenina doses herself on soma and goes to John's apartment that evening. She reproaches John for not being more excited to see her, and he responds by falling to his knees and confessing his love for her. Unable to express his feelings using his own words (words concerning "love" had never been taught to him, for not only are they socially unacceptable, but by A. F. 632, no one knows them), he falls back to Shakespeare, reciting Ferdinand's declarations of love to Miranda in *The Tempest*. He abruptly pulls away, however, as Lenina leans in to kiss him, telling her he needs to perform some sort of difficult task in order to be worthy of her. Lenina is annoyed, and John tries to explain: "At Malpais, you had to bring her the skin of a mountain lion—I mean, when you wanted to marry some one." Lenina snaps, "There aren't in lions in England." They argue, Lenina trying to make John act sensibly (i.e., give in and sleep with her), and John desperately trying to make Lenina understand his idea of romance. Lenina is finally exasperated when John starts talking about marriage and fidelity; she interrupts him and reduces everything down to a simple question: does he or doesn't he like her? John admits that he loves her "more than anything in the world," giving Lenina some relief and allowing her to embrace him. Lenina, despite John's explanations about chastity and fidelity, still sees attraction as the bottom line in the discussion—if John likes her and she likes him, there is no more to discuss. She begins to undress, prompting John to turn from Ferdinand's avowals of love to Othello's accusations of infidelity. Reacting as much to his own desire as to Lenina's sexual behavior, he calls her a whore, and an "impudent strumpet," pushing her away from him and hitting her. Terrified, she flees to his bathroom and locks herself in, begging John to slide her clothes over the door. He paces in the other room, reciting bits of *King Lear*, *Othello*, and *Troilus and Cressida* that revolve around the weakness and impurity of women. He is interrupted by a telephone call informing him that Linda has taken ill and was moved to the Park Lane Hospital for the Dying. Forgetting about Lenina in the bathroom, he rushes from the apartment, leaving Lenina to sneak out, confused and still terrified by John's scathing verbal and physical abuse.

At the Park Lane Hospital for the Dying in **chapter 14**, John is escorted to Ward 81, where Linda lies, sliding in and out of consciousness, in Bed 20. The ward is full, but Linda is the only person who shows any signs of age; progress has been such that old age descends rapidly and kills a person before they show any external signs of aging. The nurse explains to John that they try to make the hospital "something between a first-class hotel and a feely-palace"; scent and sound is kept constantly flowing through the room, and televisions are always on. John sits beside Linda's bed, crying as he remembers her, young and pretty, singing lullabies to him when he was a baby, teaching him to read as he got older, and most clearly, her telling him stories about London, "that beautiful, beautiful Other Place, whose memory, as of heaven, a paradise of goodness and loveliness, he still kept whole and intact, undefiled by contact with the reality of this real London, these actual civilized men and women."

John's tears and memories are interrupted by the entrance of a Bokanovsky group of eight-year-old Delta boys. They run through the ward as though it is their playground, but stop short at the sight of Linda, confused by her appearance. John is shocked and angered by their presence and insensitivity, and he slaps one, bringing the Head Nurse running. She threatens to throw John from the ward if he continues to interfere with the children's "death-conditioning." Interaction with the grieving and angry John would set back the children, who are slowly and consistently conditioned to associate death and the Hospital for the Dying with ice cream and fun. The Nurse lures the children away from Bed 20 with promises of chocolate eclairs.

Distracted and upset, John is unable to recall his pleasant memories of Linda from minutes before. He can now only remember images of her drunk, in bed with Popé, and being shouted at by the other boys in the pueblo. He leans toward her, desperate for her to recognize him and understand the significance of the moment, but she is lost in a soma-haze and calls him Popé. John squeezes her hand, trying to "force her to come back from this dream of ignoble pleasures ... back into the present, back into reality; the appalling present, the awful reality—but sublime, but significant, but desperately important precisely because of the imminence of that which made them so fearful." John wants Linda to acknowledge her fear of death; he does not realize this is impossible, as Linda has been conditioned, just like the children running through the ward, to see death as something natural and perhaps even lovely.

Linda reacts to his touch, again calling him Popé. Angered at her delusion and drugged acceptance of her impending death, John shakes her violently. Linda wakes up for a moment and recognizes him, but she then begins to choke, no longer able to take a breath. Panicked, John runs down the ward, calling for the nurse; by the time they reach the bed, Linda is dead. John falls to his knees and sobs uncontrollably, distressing the nurse who again worries about the possible damage to the children's conditioning. She leads them away from the mourning man, but a few boys slip away from her and stay behind. They stare curiously at Linda and at John, asking innocently and smilingly if she is dead. John pushes them away and silently leaves the hospital.

In **chapter 15**, John leaves the Park Land Hospital for the Dying at six o'clock, shift-change for the Delta menial staff. He exits the elevator into a sea of Deltas, two Bokanovsky Groups clamoring for the daily ration of soma. John is always nauseated by the sight of so many identical twins, but today, leaving the deathbed of his mother, their existence seems offensive and mocking: "Like maggots they had swarmed defilingly over the mystery of Linda's death ... they now crawled across his grief and his repentance." Miranda's words come to him yet again; "Now, suddenly, they trumpeted a call to arms. 'O brave new world!' Miranda was proclaiming the possibility of transforming even the nightmare into something fine and noble. 'O brave new world!' It was a challenge, a command." The words inspire John, and he is struck by the need for liberty: "Linda had been a slave, Linda had died; others should live in freedom, and the world be made beautiful." John pushes his way through the crowd of Deltas, screaming, "Stop! ... Listen, I beg of you ... Lend me your ears ... Don't take that horrible stuff. It's poison ..." The Deltas are confused and angry at the suggestion that they will not receive their usual dose of soma; John continues shouting at them to "throw it all away ... I come to bring you freedom." The Deputy Sub-Bursar, the authority over the crowd of Deltas and the distributor of soma, scampers to a telephone.

Back in Helmholtz's apartment, he and Bernard wonder where John could be. They are about to leave for dinner without him when Helmholtz receives a telephone call from a friend at the Park Lane Hospital for the Dying, presumably the Deputy Sub-Bursar, telling him the John has apparently gone crazy. He and Bernard rush there, arriving in time to hear John calling the uncomprehending Deltas "mewling and puking babies." He grabs the box full of soma, and to the distress of the mob, begins throwing pill-boxes out the window. The mob rushes forward, and while Bernard fearfully looks away, Helmholtz runs toward John, joining in his shouts for freedom. Bernard watches in indecision as his two friends fight the crowd, but he cannot muster the bravery to help them. His "agony of humiliated indecision" is ended when the police arrive, armed with tanks of soma-vapour, hoses of water-based anaesthetic, and a portable Synthetic Music Box playing the "Voice of Reason" and the "Voice of Good Feeling," pathetically pleading with the mob to cease their violence and love each other again. These weapons effectively quell the riot, causing the Deltas, and even John and Helmholtz, to stop fighting and instead hug one another. The Deltas are quickly give fresh pill-boxes of soma, and the police lead away John, Helmholtz, and Bernard, who protests his arrest and unsuccessfully attempts to deny his friendship with "the Savage."

In **chapter 16**, John, Helmholtz, and Bernard have been brought to Mustapha Mond's study, where they wait for him: John disinterestedly browses through the room, Helmholtz is strangely cheerful, and Bernard is terrified and silent. Mond enters and good-humoredly questions John, who admits (much to Bernard's horror) that he does not care much for "civilization." He does, however, appreciate the constant music, a comment to which the Controller responds with, "Sometimes a thousand twangling instruments will hum about my ears and sometimes voices." John is surprised and delighted by Mond's knowledge of *The Tempest*, saying, "I thought nobody knew about that book here, in England." Mond divulges that he, as a lawmaker, has the power to break the laws banning literature. John (now referred to almost exclusively as "the savage") confesses that he does not understand the reason behind banning Shakespeare, prompting Mond to lecture him in the dangers of anything old and beautiful: "Beauty's attractive, and we don't want people to be attracted by old things. We want them to like new ones." He admits that *Othello* is more beautiful than *Three Weeks in a Helicopter*, but points out that not only would *Othello* be subversive to this consumer-based, passionless society, but that society would be unable to appreciate the beauty of the play anyway (John remembers Helmholtz's reaction to Juliet's passions, and can't help but agree). Helmholtz interrupts, saying that he desires to write something as beautiful as Shakespeare, but with a story to which modern, conditioned humans could relate. Mond responds, "And it's what you will never write ... Because if it were really like *Othello* nobody could understand it, however new it might be. And if it were new, it couldn't possibly be like *Othello* ... Because our world is not the same as Othello's world. You can't make flivvers without steel—and you can't make tragedies without social instability. The world's stable now."

Mond sympathizes with John and Helmholtz, but contends that stability and happiness (modern happiness, not Shakespeare's "overcompensations for misery") are worth the price of high art and science. Helmholtz is shocked by the inclusion of science in this statement, pointing out that everyone is conditioned to believe that "science is everything." Mond, however, speaks of his own duty to censor any scientific thought that might alter society in any way, for "every change is a menace to stability." He admits that in his youth, he worked as a physicist, and was good enough to "realize that all our science is just a cookery book, with an orthodox theory of cooking that nobody's allowed to question, and a list of recipes that mustn't be added to except by special permission from the head cook." Mond's own experiments apparently towed the line between acceptable and heretical science, and he was finally given the choice between being exiled to an island, or becoming a World Controller and giving up his own scientific quest for the truth in exchange for the power to keep the masses stable and happy. Obviously, he chose the second option, but admits that at times, he wonders whether he would have been happier on an island after all, where he could have met "the most interesting set of men and women to be found anywhere in the world. All the people who, for one reason or another, have got too self-consciously individual to fit into community-life." In fact, the Controller acknowledges that a part of him envies Helmholtz for his impending exile.

This talk of exile proves too much for Bernard, who becomes hysterical and has to be subdued (with soma) and carried to another room by four of Mond's secretaries. Helmholtz, however, is excited at the prospect of living on an island, having the freedom to pursue individual ideas and associate with others who have not been totally shaped by their conditioning. Mond offers him a choice of islands, suggesting that perhaps he would prefer a tropical, or mild island. Sounding more like John than a civilized Londoner, Helmholtz answers: "I should like a thoroughly bad climate ... I believe one would write better if the climate were bad. If there were a lot of wind and storms, for example...." Helmholtz will be exiled to the Falkland Islands.

Dignified and inspired in the face of his impending exile, Helmholtz leaves Mond's study to check on Bernard in **chapter 17**. John and Mond are finally alone, and Huxley indulges in a debate between their two positions—viviparous versus engineered life—disguised as a conversation.

Still smarting from his mother's death, and completely disillusioned with the "brave new world," John bitingly reminds the Controller that stability and continuous happiness comes with the price tag of art and science. Mond agrees with John, and perhaps a bit nostalgically mentions that religion must also be abandoned. Mond attempts to explain the concept of God to the savage, but soon realizes that John probably understands God and religion better than he, as he grew up on a Reservation where worship was central to the community (recall John's devastation when he is not allowed to undergo the mystical coming-of-age ritual with the other boys). Mond's knowledge comes from literary artifacts; in his safe there is a well-worn copy of the Holy Bible, as well as copies of other religious texts and theological treatises. Mond laughs: "A whole collection of pornographic old books. God in the safe and Ford on the shelves." John is appalled that Mond has the knowledge of God (which John seems to believe is the ultimate unquestionable) but withholds it from the populace, a position Mond is quick to defend. He explains that, as with *Othello*, the world would not understand the Bible, that it concerns "God hundreds of years ago. Not about God now ... Men [change]." Mond attempts to explain with the writings of Cardinal Newman and Maine de Biran ("Cardinal" and "philosopher" being terms John can define only using quotations from Shakespeare. Newman argues that "independence was not made for man—that it is an unnatural state—will do for a while, but will not carry us on safely to the end," while Maine suggests that "the religious sentiment tends to develop as we grow older; to develop because, as the passions grow calm, as the fancy and sensibilities are less excited and excitable, our reason becomes less troubled in its working, less obscured by the images, desires and distractions, in which is used to be absorbed." Mond uses these arguments to justify why religion would be out of place in the modern world, where there *is* no old age, no passions to dim, and no excitable youth to entertain the idea of independent existence. There is simply no basis for religious belief in A. F. 632. Mond punctuates this by admitting that he believes there is a God: "[now] he manifests himself as an absence."

John valiantly attempts to find an argument for the introduction of religion into this world of eugenics and mind-control, but Mond counters him at every point. God would allow man a reason for "bearing things patiently"; but now there is nothing to bear. God would give a reason for self-denial; but "industrial civilization is only possible when there's no self-denial." God would be a reason for chastity; but stability would crumble under the weight of passion that chastity would introduce. God would be the reason for heroism and nobility of soul; but heroism and virtue thrive on conflict, and without wars there need be no heroes.

Nearly defeated, John finally quotes *Hamlet*: "What you need is something *with* tears for a change. Nothing costs enough here ... Exposing what is mortal and unsure to all that fortune, death and danger dare, even for an eggshell. Isn't there something in that? ... Quite apart from God—though of course God would be a reason for it. Isn't there something in living dangerously?" Mond quickly agrees, yes there is an enormous benefit to the rush of adrenaline; hence the mandatory monthly Violent Passion Surrogate, which physically simulates the effects of all of the passion eliminated by soma and conditioning. "All the tonic effects of murdering Desdemona and being murdered by Othello, without any of the inconveniences."

John insists that he craves the inconveniences: "I don't want comfort. I want God, I want poetry, I want real danger, I want freedom, I want goodness. I want sin." Mond reminds him that with these things, he is also stuck with old age, disease, starvation, fear, torture, and a multitude of other horrors. "I claim them all" is John's only response. There is no further argument; the savage and the Controller understand each other, but ultimately they disagree at the heart of the issue. John wants to make the decision Mond chose not to so many years ago; he wants individuality instead of stability.

In **chapter 18**, Helmholtz and Bernard visit John to say their farewells. They are surprised to find him vomiting, the result of a "purification ritual he has imposed on himself, drinking mustard mixed with warm water. Astonished, they ask if he ate something rancid; he replies: "I ate civilization ... It poisoned me; I was defiled. And then ... I ate my own wickedness." In the face of his approaching exile, Bernard has regained some of his self-respect, and bravely apologizes to John for his behavior at the party. John and Helmholtz silence him; the situation has allied the three of them beyond what now seem like insignificant personal spats. John tells the two men that he asked to be sent to the Falkland Islands with them, but that the

Controller refused, saying "he wanted to go on with the experiment." John is furious as he recounts the decision, asserting that he refuses to "experimented with" and shall run away "anywhere ... so long as I can be alone."

The chapter skips forward and unspecified amount of time (not too long, presumably), and John has fled London. He decides to take up hiding in an abandoned lighthouse only 15 minutes by air to London, but sufficiently isolated since it was no longer near the fields of any country games, so completely removed from the life of nature-hating population. Before he sleeps in the lighthouse, he spends a night purifying himself (by prayer and voluntary crucifixion, much as he described to Bernard soon after they met) so that he is worthy of the "almost too comfortable" ferro-concrete structure. He intends to spend the rest of life in total solitude, living off of a garden (he brought seeds with him) and wild game; one of his first chores is constructing a bow and arrows out of a nearby ash tree. Note Huxley's choice of tree: the ash is identified in mythologies from many cultures, including Norse and Greek. Its' sweet manna is often recognized as a (sometimes) supernatural intoxicant, and sometimes is even referred to as "soma." While whittling ash branches for a bow, John realizes that he is singing to himself, and in punishment for his enjoyment, mixes his mustard-water to purge. Following this internal purification, John fashions a whip out of knotted cords, and beats himself to the point of drawing blood and beyond. Unfortunately, this display was witnessed by three Delta-Minuses, inexplicably driving instead of taking public transportation. They are shocked and rush off, but John's isolation is over.

Three days after John's unwitting display, reporters descend on his lighthouse, anxious to interview him. Not surprisingly, John kicks a reporter, prompting the others to maintain a certain distance, but this does not discourage them from harassing him from afar. He finally shoots a homemade arrow into a hovering helicopter, and is seemingly left alone.

It is not long before John finds another excuse to whip himself into purification; this time he is appalled by lustful thoughts of Lenina, whom he last saw naked and willing in his apartment before he screamed at her in rage and frightened her into taking refuge in his bathroom. John does not realize that an "expert big game photographer" had been camping out near the lighthouse for three days, laying microphones, wires and cameras in the hope that John would put on another savage display. He captures John's entire self-inflicted punishment on film, and it is released as a Feelie a mere twelve days later—*The Savage of Surrey*. The popularity of the real-life footage prompts a renewed interest in John's savage lifestyle, and his property is swarmed by workers desperate to catch a glimpse of the Savage beating himself in a frenzy. They ignore his shouts, delighting in his anger as he begs them to leave, ecstatic when he picks up the now-famous whip and waves it threateningly (there is, however, nothing he can really do against so many). The circus is interrupted by the arrival of Lenina (accompanied by Henry Foster), who steps toward John with her arms open as though to embrace him. He snaps, and rushes at her, screaming "Strumpet" and "Fitchew," as usual relaying on Shakespeare to vent his most passionate feelings. The mob shrieks, "Let's see the whipping stunt," and is rapturous as John begins to whip Lenina; they close in tighter, desperate to touch the Savage and witness his wildness first-hand. John turns the whip on his own body, shouting "Oh, the flesh! Kill it, kill it!"

"Drawn by the fascination of the horror of pain, from within, impelled by that habit of cooperation, that desire for unanimity and atonement, which their conditioning had so ineradicably implanted in them, they began to mime the frenzy of his gestures, striking at one another as the Savage struck at his own rebellious flesh, or at that plump incarnation of turpitude writhing in the heather at his feet." As the mob attacks itself, someone sings "Orgy-Porgy," and what had been a violent frenzy morphs into a religious/sexual Solidarity Song.

Caught up in the orgy, John is also swept along in a soma-induced passion. After midnight, the mob finally disperses, leaving John to sleep off his "long-drawn frenzy of sexuality." He wakes, alone, the following morning, and is shamed by the memory of his loss of control.

Reporters, desperate for more information about the previous night's "orgy of atonement" (as it was dubbed by the press), descend on the lighthouse that afternoon. John is nowhere to be seen, and they enter the building. There they discover his body, dangling slowly back and forth, as it hangs from the second floor. John has lost his loss of control, which he views has a loss of principle, morals, and most importantly, discipline. He has tasted soma and engaged in the most sacred of Fordian customs (the orgy/impromptu Solidarity Service), and he seems to have enjoyed it. But this behavior, and especially the enjoyment of this behavior, is unacceptable to John's unconditioned mind, and perhaps finally realizing the hopelessness of his situation—that he is neither a member of London society or the reservation—John commits suicide.

# Critical Views

PETER BOWERING ON HUXLEY'S USE OF SOMA

After ectogenesis and conditioning, Soma was the most powerful instrument of authority in the hands of the Controllers of the World-State. Huxley had already speculated on the invention of a new drug, a more efficient and less harmful substitute for alcohol and cocaine; he considered that if he were a millionaire, he would endow a band of research workers to look for the ideal intoxicant. The rulers of *Brave New World*, with a similar object in mind, had subsidized two thousand pharmacologists and biochemists to search for the perfect drug. Soma was the product of six years' research; euphoric, narcotic, pleasantly hallucinant, it had all the advantages of alcohol and none of the defects, but there the resemblance ended. To the inhabitants of Huxley's utopia the Soma habit was not a private vice but a political institution. The World Controllers encouraged the systematic drugging of their own citizens for the benefit of the state.

> The daily Soma ration was an insurance against personal maladjustment, social unrest and the spread of subversive ideas. Religion, Karl Marx declared, is the opium of the people. In the Brave New World this situation was reversed. Opium, or rather Soma, was the people's religion. Like religion, the drug had power to console and compensate, it called up visions of another, better world, it offered hope, strengthened faith and promoted charity. (*Brave New World Revisited*, ch. viii)

Huxley, comparing his novel with *1984*, observes that in the latter a strict code of sexual morality is imposed on the party hierarchy. The society of Orwell's fable is permanently at war and therefore aims to keep its subjects in a constant state of tension. A puritanical approach to sex is therefore a major instrument of policy. The World-State, however, of *Brave New*

World is one in which war has been eliminated and the first aim of its rulers is to keep their subjects from making trouble. Together with Soma, sexual licence, made practical by the abolition of the family, is one of the chief means of guaranteeing the inhabitants against any kind of destructive or creative emotional tension. The appalling dangers of family life had first been pointed out by Our Ford or 'Our Freud, as, for some inscrutable reason, he chose to call himself whenever he spoke of psychological matters' (ch. iii). Once the world had been full of every kind of perversion from chastity to sadism; but the World Controllers had realized that an industrial civilization depended on self-indulgence. Chastity meant passion and neurasthenia, and passion and neurasthenia meant instability, which, in turn, meant a constant threat to civilization. Therefore life for Brave New Worlders was made emotionally easy; in short, people were saved from having any emotions at all. No one was allowed to love anyone too much; there were no temptations to resist, and if something unpleasant were to happen, there was always Soma. Legalized sexual freedom was made possible by every device known to applied science. Contraceptive precautions were prescribed by the regulations while years of 'intensive hypnopaedia and, from twelve to seventeen, Malthusian drill three times a week had made the taking of these precautions almost as automatic and inevitable as blinking' (ch. v).

Soma and licensed promiscuity would probably have been sufficient in themselves to prevent the Brave New Worlders from taking any active interest in the realities of the social and political situation; circuses, however, are a traditional aid to dictators, and the Controllers of the World-State were no exception. Instead of spending their leisure hours working out the practical implications of the theory of relativity, like their predecessors in (H. G. Wells's) *Men Like Gods*, Huxley's utopians were provided with a series of non-stop distractions guaranteed to ward off boredom and discourage idle speculation about the nature of things. Any frustrated religious instincts were provided for by the Ford's Day Solidarity Services, where, in a crude parody of the Holy Communion, dedicated Soma Tablets and the loving cup of ice-cream Soma were passed round. By these means the Controllers insured that the Brave New Worlders loved their servitude and never dreamt of revolution.

JEROME MECKIER ON HUXLEY'S IRONIC UTOPIA

That Huxley should have written even one utopia is, from one point of view, very surprising. His early novels often seemed concerned mainly with exploding outworn ideas and revealing the mutual contradictoriness of modern alternatives. Readers of *Brave New World* invariably point to Mr. Scogan's comments in *Crome Yellow* as an indication of Huxley's perennial concern with the future. Indeed, Scogan, a gritty rationalist, could sue the author of *Brave New World*, for it contains little that he did not foresee. Scogan may, in fact, be a caricature of H. G. Wells, and it is thus intentionally ironic that his view of the future contrasts with his prehistoric appearance as a bird-lizard with an incisive beaked nose, dry and scaly skin, and the hands of a crocodile. Scogan predicts that, in the future. population will be obtained and controlled through bottle-breeding and the use of incubators. The family system, he continues, 'will disappear' and Eros will be pursued without fear of consequences. At times he waxes lyrical over the prospect of 'the Rational State' wherein each child, properly classified by mind and temperament, will be duly 'labelled and docketed' for the education that will best enable him and his species 'to perform those functions which human beings of his variety are capable of performing'. Even the one prediction Scogan is less specific about is relevant. He complains that 'For us', virtual prisoners of society and its impositions, 'a complete holiday is out of the question'. He may not envision soma itself, but he is aware of his Rational State's need for it.

However, despite what Scogan says in his capacity as a twentieth-century extension of the nineteenth-century progress-oriented reformer, Huxley's early prose is full of utopian disclaimers in which he greets the idea of writing a utopia with contempt. In one of his earliest remarks about utopian writers, Huxley condemns them, as he condemns most of his own characters, for escapism and eccentricity, for an egoistic inability to accept reality as they find it: Outward reality disgusts them; the compensatory dream is the universe in which they live. The subject of their meditations is not man, but a monster of rationality and virtue—of one kind of rationality and virtue at that, their own. *Brave New World* is a 'monster of rationality' in which the rational is raised to an irrational power until, for example, the goal of sanitation reform in the nineteenth century, namely cleanliness, replaces godliness. Unfortunately, Huxley's comment about monsters of rationality also applies, eventually, to his own *Island*.

What Huxley's anti-utopian remarks in the late 1920s boil down to, then, is a hatred of the utopian speculations he was reading, or had read by 1930. Most of these, taking their cue from H. G. Wells, and ultimately from Bacon's *New Atlantis* (1627), were scientific. Those who foresee a utopian future, Huxley wrote, 'invoke not the god from the machine, but the machine itself'. Huxley's spoofing of the Wellsian notion that people in utopia should take turns doing high-brow and low-brow tasks: 'While Jones plays the piano, Smith spreads the manure' was just a preliminary for the full-fledged satire of *Brave New World*.

Thus although in one sense Huxley's novels and non-fiction prose prior to 1932 seemed to indicate that he would never stoop to utopian themes, in another they made *Brave New World* inevitable. One of the chief reasons why Huxley wrote the novel, it is tempting to conclude, was to discredit, if not discourage, the sort of utopian writing he was familiar with. The urge to write a literary satire on existing works went hand in hand with the desire to challenge, by means of a correcting, less optimistic vision of his own, the picture of the future that science was enthusiastically offering. In his prose essays, Huxley was thus composing Brave New World for years before starting the novel itself. In essays from *Music at Night*, such as 'Liberty and the Promised Land', 'History and the Past', 'Wanted a New Pleasure', and throughout *Proper Studies*,

Huxley was indulging in distopian prose, from which the anti-utopian or distopian novel and eventually the positive utopia spring almost inevitably. The difference between the satirist and the writer of utopias is somewhat minimal to begin with, since the second, like the first, intends to expose the difference between what he beholds and what he would prefer to see. Once the anti-utopian novel is written, its counterpart already exists by implication. As Huxley became increasingly convinced that he had found the true path, he employed the medium of a positive utopia to explore a future of his own conceiving. Eventually, Huxley, too, disclosed his compensatory dream.

Even the anti-utopian non-fiction prose just mentioned, however, is hardly free of moments when Huxley is possibly not ridiculing scientific utopias, when he seems, instead, intrigued by their possibility—an attitude which often makes the reader suspect that *Brave New World* is not the total satire some critics claim. The question of 'eugenic reform' always has a fascination for Huxley. He entertains it in *Music at Night* as a means of raising the critical point beyond which increases in prosperity, leisure, and education now give diminishing returns. He even speaks, with apparent tolerance, of a new caste system based on differences in native ability and of an educational process that supplies an individual with just so much instruction as his position calls for. He worries, in *Proper Studies*, about the threat to the world's IQ that the more rapidly reproducing inferior classes constitute. And when, in an essay catalogued above as distopian prose, he predicts that society 'will learn to breed babies in bottles', or talks, albeit somewhat critically, of theatres wherein 'egalitarians' will enjoy talkies, tasties, smellies, and feelies, he almost seems to become Scogan.

Huxley is even more eloquent than Scogan on the possibilities of a holiday-inducing drug when he writes that: 'If we could sniff or swallow something that would, for five or six hours each day, abolish our solitude as individuals ... earth would become paradise.' What Scogan wanted was an escape hatch, but what Huxley wants is a means of breaking down the individual's isolation within his own ego. The difference between the two positions, however, is not so clear as to make pointing it out unnecessary. The drug called soma in *Brave New World* is not inherently unsatisfactory, but rather is an inadequate surrogate for something Huxley would accept in a more proper form.

LAURENCE BRANDER ON THE "MASS COMMUNITY"

It is our modern preoccupation with social and political insanity which colours our modern Utopias, and makes *Brave New World* and *1984* so different even from the satirical Utopias which went before. It is ironic that when at last all men could be properly housed, clothed and fed, we are teetering on the edge of an almost universal destruction and conduct our affairs with apparently irremediable lunacy. It may be that our knowledge explosion with its shattering technical progress, has knocked us off balance and when we recover we shall succeed in imposing control. It may be that the natural balance in human affairs requires that great advances imply equally great dangers. When Huxley and Orwell wrote their Utopias, western man was struggling in the deepest trough of his despair. It seemed that the mental and spiritual life of mankind was so distorted that it could never recover. It was difficult in those decades to see any hope for the human race and their visions give typical pictures of our despair.

In *Brave New World* Huxley is facing particularly the fear of overpopulation, which since then has become a nightmare. In 'The Double Crisis,' an essay published in *Themes and Variations* (1950) he says: 'The human race is passing through a time of crisis, and that crisis exists, so to speak, on two levels—an upper level of political and economic crisis and a lower level of demographic and ecological crisis.' He goes on to argue that the one affects the other and offers sensible solutions. It is a very living problem and has been so for a long time. Even in the twenties, the press of people on the earth was noticeable and it was apparent that they were forming a mass. What passes for education had made them so an as early as 1915 Wilfrid Trotter had demonstrated the necessity for new techniques of mass management in his *Conduct of the Herd in Peace and War*. The most eloquent analysis of the situation was offered by Ortega y Gasset in his *Revolt of the Masses* (1930). 'Europe', he says in his opening sentences, 'is suffering from the greatest crisis that can afflict peoples, nations and civilisation.' He was not thinking of the coming war in Spain or the still more dreadful conflict which was to unsettle the world. He was thinking of population. 'Towns are full of people, houses full of tenants, hotels full of guests, trains full of travellers, cafés full of customers, parks full of promenaders, consulting-rooms of famous doctors full of patients, theatres full of spectators, and beaches full of bathers. What previously was, in general, no problem, now begins to be an every day one, namely, to find room.'

Huxley and Orwell face the problem of ruling these masses. They look at what we have made of our English democracy and substitute for that a satirical insanity much more odious. Orwell produced a sick man's nightmare of sadism based on his observations of European totalitarianisms. Huxley wrote out of his scientific background and mass-produced his population in the fashion long popular in science fiction, growing them in bottles and conditioning them from birth in all the ways proposed by psychologists. Both heredity and environment were absolutely determined. These bottle products were released from moral tensions because they were so conditioned that none of their actions had moral consequences. They could always escape from reality very easily by the use of the standard drug, soma, which was a great improvement on alcohol or anything else known because it produced no unpleasant reactions and was benignly addictive. The people were always in a state of euphoria because the human spirit had been prisoned and confined in a perfectly conditioned healthy cadaver. 'And that', put in the Director sententiously, 'that is the secret of happiness and virtue—liking what you've got to do. All conditioning aims at that: making people like their inescapable social destiny.'

The old trouble in human societies, that some are more equal than others, has been resolved. The population problem has been resolved. People are manufactured as they are needed, a few Alpha Plus specimens, hundreds of Epsilons. It is fascinating, because as in all these satires, it is a twist of known data, with the creative spirit working at white heat pursuing every absurdity the original twist suggests. The normal is the extravagant and outrageous and once the reader has been conditioned to accept this inverted normalcy, opposition is introduced to make the tale. Accidents happen when the bottles are in production and that gives us two high intelligence characters who are misfits. A little alcohol accidently splashed into the bottle, perhaps. The story wants something more, so the Savage is introduced. He was born viviparously, out of a careless Beta Minus who had gone with an Alpha Plus male on a trip to the native reservation, one of the settlements of old type human beings still in existence. A pregnant Beta Minus could not possibly be brought back to England, so she stays to give birth to a son and supports him by prostitution. He is a young man when we meet him, with a strong individuality stimulated by reading Shakespeare; just the opposition the story requires, a romantic idealist in a controlled society.

The purpose of the book is to give us a full picture of a society scientifically manufactured and controlled and the story is a means to that end. If any reader flags, he will be sexually titillated. Orwell used the same device. Huxley is creating a country according to the prophet Ford, who developed mass production. 'Standard men and women in uniform batches.' Electric shocks when babies, crawl towards pretty flowers or pretty pictures: 'saved from books and botany all their lives.' Erotic play in children encouraged; they will be young for all the sixty years of their lives and enormously potent, and in this will lie their natural happiness. The women will never conceive and everyone can and should be completely promiscuous. It would be unnatural and unsocial to go steady. There are no families and there is no mother love. What we call friendship develops only between the misfits. Average citizens lived under the influence of soma all their lives and therefore without individuality or integrity. In 1932 Huxley thought this was a remote nightmare but already in 1946 he confessed that his brave new world was coming quicker than he had expected.

The core of the book is the argument on happiness between the Controller and the Savage. They argue like a couple of Oxford dons on the name and nature of happiness in society. The Savage reveals a power in dialectic for which his past life, one would have thought, had hardly prepared him. Huxley is right. It would have been better if the Savage had had another background, something worth preferring. As it is, he has to choose between the squalor of the Reservation and the spiritless shallow happiness of the world according to Ford. He tried to find another alternative. He sought solitude and silence in a disused lighthouse on the south coast. Despite his continued study of Shakespeare he could not get away from thoughts of Lenina. Huxley later confessed in *Texts and Pretexts* a small slip there: 'I wanted this person to be a platonic lover; but, reading through the plays, I realized to my dismay that platonic love is not a subject with which Shakespeare ever deals.' The Savage flagellates himself to subdue the flesh. He is observed. All the resources of mass communication go into operation and very soon hordes of the public descend upon him. Among them is Lenina, the fair temptress. The Savage makes the escape of the creature that is hurt too much; he kills himself.

It is the parable of the individual in the mass community. We live in the age of the mass. The politicians, the salesmen, the entertainers, all who batten on the mass exacerbate the instincts which sway human beings as a mass. The decent individual is carried along, still protesting but more than ever lost. In our timid totalitarianism the individual is bruised and frustrated by forces as impersonal as nature herself. In *Brave New World* and *1984* the implacable scrutiny of the state is directed on them all the time. The 'proles' are easily controlled; it is the individualistic party member who can cause trouble, the misfit Bernard and the pitiful Winston. With individuals so marked, dynamic progress becomes impossible and both these books present us with the static state. As such states have always crashed, Huxley and Orwell are at pains to explain how the rulers secured stability.

Stability in a community is based upon organic progress and in his 1946 Foreword Huxley would offer the Savage as a reasonable alternative to a totalitarian state according to the enlightened visions of nineteenth-century Europe. Anything else surrounds us with muddle. He concludes his suggested revision with something from a different world of thought; he introduces the idea of the 'intelligent pursuit of man's Final End, the unitive knowledge of the immanent Tao or Logos'. (We recall that *The Perennial Philosophy* was published in the same year.) This completely changes the totalitarian version of the Greatest Happiness principle back towards something as old as the Hindu caste system, which catered for the evolution of the individual until he was fit to become part of the Whole. A complete contrast to the grubby materialist totalitarianism towards which our masses are dragging us.

PETER FIRCHOW ON SATIRICAL VERSUS FUTURISTIC READINGS

Equally important, especially for a proper understanding of *Brave New World*, Huxley almost certainly never intended his novel to be a satire of the future. For what, after all, is the good of satirizing the future? The only meaningful future is actually, as he observed in an essay published a year earlier, the future which already exists in the present. "O brave new world," let us remember, is what Miranda exclaims when she sees for the first time the as yet unredeemed inhabitants of the *old* world, an irony of which Huxley is fully aware. The present is what matters most in *Brave New World*, as it does in any good Utopia; and Huxley only uses the lens of future time (as preceding satirists had often resorted to geographical or past remoteness) in order to discover better the latent diseases of the here and now.*

Looking back at the novel after a lapse of fifteen years, Huxley once suggested (what should really be obvious to everyone and what differentiates this novel so radically from vaguely similar but inferior works by other authors) that the theme of the novel is "not the advancement of science as such; it is the advancement of science as it affects human individuals."[1] This is a problem which had been growing increasingly acute since the great scientific avalanche of the late nineteenth and early twentieth centuries (hence Helmholtz, Bernard and Watson as names for some of the main characters in the novel), and which. after the First World War and the Soviet Revolution, had assumed ever more oppressive political and economic forms (therefore Lenina, Marx, and Mond).** Huxley had been charting the course of this sort of scientific progress for the last decade, particularly in its guises of psychology, political propaganda, and their popular corollary, advertising. In this sense, *Brave New World* is a direct descendant of *Antic Hay*. The world of A.F. 632 is simply the thoroughgoing realization of the ideal of the Complete Man, a never ending round of good times. Like the Complete Man's world, this world is basically materialistic and sensual—only more so. The result of this intensification of "happiness" is that there exists almost no possibility for the completer man to discard his beard, listen to Mozart instead of the Sixteen Sexophonists, or choose to enter a "crystal world" instead of an orgy-porgian Solidarity Service. In the name of a totally external happiness, any kind of significant internal life has been banished from the Fordian world.

The intensity with which Huxley felt *Brave New World* to be an attack on the present or on the present as contained in the future can be seen from his repeated attempts to gauge the progress of the malady of dehumanization.*** When he took its temperature in an article written for *Life* magazine in 1948, the great blights of fascism, the Second World War, and the atom bomb had intervened to alter the condition of mankind and therefore Huxley's diagnosis. Now he maintained that, instead of one, there were two myths underlying the psyche and behavior of Western man. To the myth of progress he added the myth of nationalism, the former promulgated through the medium of advertising, the latter through political propaganda and brainwashing.[2] From this we can see—though Huxley did not explicitly make the connection—that in the new world the myth of nationalism with its accompanying propaganda has disappeared because of the massive destruction of the Nine Years' War (as Mustapha Mond instructs the Savage) and because the instruments of technological blandness have triumphed over those of nationalistic brutality; indeed, the plot of the novel (such as it is) consists of a reenactment of this triumph in miniature. On the other hand, in *Ape and Essence*, which Huxley was working on as he wrote the *Life* essay, it is apparent that the myth of progress has been displaced by a religious variant of nationalism. The stupidity of both of these myths, according to Huxley, is that they stress the external aspects of life, not the internal. Their disciples, therefore, must inevitably "progress" to one or another kind of perdition: the perdition of "heaven" or the perdition of hell. Hence, this kind of progress is really no progress at all. Real progress, in Huxley's terms, can only be defined as "personal progress," or "internal, progress." It is only through this type of advancement that one can hope to create a "genuinely human society," and only such a society can assure the continued existence of genuine human individuals, not diabolically happy or diabolically unhappy animals.

Notes

1. The 1946 preface to the novel reprinted in the *Collected Works Edition*, p. x.

2. Aldous Huxley, "Brave New World," *Life*, 25 (September 20, 1948), 63–64, 66–68, 70.

* Another example of an anti-Utopia which uses a projection into the future to satirize the present is the Russian novelist Zamiatin's *We*. This work is occasionally mentioned as an influence on *Brave New World*, but Zamiatin's connection with *1984* seems more immediate.

In quite another, and rather more trivial, sense *Brave New World* is also an attack on the present's conception of the future. Specifically, it is a parody of H. G. Wells's optimistic fantasy of the future, *Men like Gods*. This is confirmed by Huxley in a letter dated May 18, 1931: "I am writing a novel about the future—on the horror of the Wellsian Utopia and a revolt against it" (L348). In *Private History* (London, 1960), p. 154, Derek Patmore relates how Wells reacted to this revolt: "Ever an ardent socialist, he was certain that social progress would cure the evils that men were so easily prone to, and when we discussed the works of such writers as Aldous Huxley he said to me savagely: '*Brave New World* was a great disappointment to me. A writer of the standing of Aldous Huxley has no right to betray the future as he did in that book. When thinking about the future, people seem to overlook the logical progress in education, in architecture, and science.'"

** Some of the future developments of science as presented in this novel, in particular the idea of the baby hatcheries, are derived from J. B. S. Haldane's *Daedalus, or Science and the Future* (London, 1924). For a discussion of this work, see Ronald Clark's *JBS*.

*** The most thorough reexamination is to be found in *Brave New World Revisited* (London, 1939).

IRA GRUSHOW ON *BRAVE NEW WORLD* AND *THE TEMPEST*

One play of Shakespeare's, however, *The Tempest*, bears a more intimate relationship to *Brave New World* than the others. Huxley has taken his title, of course, from Miranda's exclamation upon meeting the party of the King of Naples, the first men other than her father Prospero and her betrothed Ferdinand whom she has ever seen:

> O wonder!
> How many goodly creatures are there here!
> How beauteous mankind is! O brave new world,
> That has such people in't!

John Savage repeats these words several times in the course of the novel, first when he learns that Bernard Marx intends to take him back with him to civilization. As in Shakespeare (Alonso, Sebastian, and Antonio are, after all, plotters, usurpers, and would-be assassins) the words "O brave new world!" are ironic. John, no less than Miranda, is in for a few surprises when he gets to civilization. His education has not prepared him for the world outside the reservation, just as Miranda's education, one feels strangely apprehensive, may not be wholly adequate for a princess of Naples. Huxley's book may be said to begin where Shakespeare's play leaves off. Just as W. H. Auden, in *The Sea and the Mirror*, has explored the thoughts and feelings of the characters of *The Tempest* on their boat trip from the enchanted island back to Naples, so Huxley treats of the reaction of John Savage, a type of Miranda, to the world of "civilized" men and women.

The irony of John's exclamation, "O brave new world," pervades the whole relationship of Huxley's novel to Shakespeare's play, and even after the reader has accepted the fact of reference to *The Tempest*, he may not readily see the identifications that Huxley makes. It is not immediately apparent, for example, that Bernard Marx represents Caliban, the deformed monster and unwilling slave of Prospero, described by his master as "a devil, a born devil, on whose nature / Nurture can never stick; on whom my pains, / Humanely taken, are all lost, quite lost." But the resemblance is unmistakable. Like Caliban's, Marx's questionable birth, or decanting, is against him, his physical deformity breeds discontent and rebellion, and his education or conditioning has failed to produce its desired results. "You taught me language," Caliban upbraids his master, "and my profit on't / Is, I know how to curse; the red plague rid you, / For learning me your language!" So might Bernard Marx rail against the hypnopaedic instruction he has been subjected to. Again, like Caliban, Marx takes part in an unsuccessful insurrection, and, terrified of his master's wrath, he abjectly begs for mercy when the plot is covered.

If Marx is Caliban, then who is the Savage? We have already established that one of his functions in the novel is to play the role that Miranda might have in a sequel to *The Tempest*. He is the innocent suddenly brought into an evil world. But as Lenina's virtuous lover he identifies himself with Ferdinand as well. Like Ferdinand's, John's sorrow for the loss of a parent is gradually displaced by a love which is not filial. Like Ferdinand, John believes in taking a bride, not for the asking, but by winning her through the accomplishment of some arduous task. He quotes Ferdinand to the effect that "some kinds of baseness / Are nobly undergone." And again like Ferdinand, John is committed to strict chastity before marriage. At one point the Savage quotes Prospero's injunction to Ferdinand:

> If thou dost break her virgin knot before
> All sanctimonious ceremonies may
> With full and holy rite be minister'd
> No sweet aspersion shall the heavens let fall
> To make this contract grow....

John also quotes Ferdinand's assurance that

> The most opportune place, the strong'st suggestion
> Our worser genius can, shall never melt
> Mine honour into lust....

It is, of course, one of the bitterest morsels of Huxley's irony that John can only speak for himself. If he represents Ferdinand, then Lenina must be Miranda. The measure of the difference between Shakespeare's fresh, innocent, intelligent virgin and Huxley's jaded, experienced, automated Alpha is the full measure of the difference between Shakespeare's vision of an ideal world and Huxley's. The confused exchange of dialogue between John and Lenina in the scene where she tries to seduce him once more enforces linguistically the incompatibility of their two worlds.

If Lenina represents an unreluctant Miranda, then her father is Prospero. But a properly decanted female Alpha of A.F. 632 has no parent of either sex. As the law regards certain persons not progenitors as acting *in loco parentis*, however, so may we consider the Controller, Mustapha Mond, as a father-surrogate to Lenina and, indeed, to all under his care. Through his planning and coordination their generation has been brought about, and through his direction and supervision their conditioning has been effected. Moreover, like Prospero in the play, the Controller is the guiding figure in Huxley's novel: he knows what is going on at all times and he determines the fate of all those under his dominion. His wrath is fearful: just as Caliban cringes before Prospero, so does Marx before Mustapha Mond. But here again there is a gross distortion of character. Mond is a Prospero who has elected to stay in Milan, a Prospero who for the sake of security and worldly power has renounced his scientific studies. Given a choice (as in a sense Shakespeare's Prospero was) of getting on in the world or of continuing his quest for truth, Mond does not choose as Prospero does. And as in Shakespeare so in Huxley an island, remote from all commerce with the rest of the world, is the only escape open to the nonconforming thinker.

PETER M. LARSEN ON HUXLEY'S USE OF "SYNTHETIC MYTHS"

It is necessary to distinguish between *analytic* and *synthetic* myths.[2] The analytic myth makes a statement about an opposition, and describes the conflict and the opposition which it mediates. Thus, analytic myth exists synchronically in the form of fictional or relational narrative. The synthetic myth is the mediator divorced from the opposition which generated it, i.e. an incontrovertible statement. Thus, 'everyone belongs to everyone else' (*BNW*, pp. 42, 45, 47 100, 105, 162) is a synthetic myth mediating a hidden emotional conflict inherent in a society where it is evident that nobody belongs to anybody or anything.[3]

One problem to a discussion of synthetic myth is due to the fact that the actual process of mediation is obscured; at best, one can hope to reconstruct the process, and present a speculative explanation of it. The synthetic myth often grows out of an original analytic myth during a period of numerous repetitions; the mediator can disengage itself from its analytic context and acquire a formulaic, proverb-like status. Behind the jingle 'When the individual feels, the community reels' (*BNW*, p. 80), one must assume an analytic mythic narrative which explains why this is so. And as a matter of fact, Mustapha Mond, 'Resident Controller for Western Europe', provides us with one version of the myth, split up in a larger context (*ibid.*, pp. 38–54), and states 'No civilization without social stability. No social stability without individual stability' (*ibid.*, p. 44). This 'explanation' is naturally reserved for Alphas, the most intelligent caste, and is in most cases unnecessary even for them. The synthetic myth is typically geared for reiteration, and does not provide intellectual, but only moral knowledge. In *BNW* the individual is hypnopaedically conditioned and given a moral education which 'ought never, in any circumstances, to be rational' (*BNW*, p. 32) The end result is that the synthetic myths become powerful ideological tools, and 'axiomatic, self-evident, utterly indisputable' (*ibid.* p. 42).[4] It is important to note that an ideology, in this case an ideology of happiness, can exploit synthetic myths to maintain its own interests, and to conceal the internal conflicts which arise between the interests of society and those of the individual.

In *BNW*, the synthetic myths can be divided into five groups: jingles, rewritten nursery rhymes, rewritten proverbs, new proverbs and pseudostatements. All are types of discourse designed for parroting, i.e., meaningless rhythmic repetition, and so in keeping with the infantile emotionalism of society in 632 A[fter] F[ord] The jingles, e.g., 'Ending is better than mending' (*BNW*, pp. 49, 50, 51), or 'a gramme is better than a damn' (*ibid.*, pp. 53, 78, 96, 154), are tailored for easy remembrance, and are only marginally different from advertising slogans in our society.[5] Jingles and slogans age quickly and are replaced by new ones, the point is made in *BNW* where it is mentioned that Helmholtz Watson 'had the happiest knack for slogans and hypnopaedic rhymes' (*ibid.*, p. 61) suggesting that to fact, his job is to write endless reams of advertising copy.

The nursery rhymes, e.g., 'Orgy-porgy' (*BNW*, pp. 73, 74, 146, 200) or 'A, B, C, Vitamin D' (*ibid.*, pp. 110, 159, 160–61), stress the social infantilism, and serve a satiric purpose for the perceptive reader. The rewritten proverbs, e.g., 'Ford helps those who help themselves' (*ibid.*, p. 168) or 'What man has joined, nature is powerless to put asunder' (*ibid.*, p. 29), are satirical in the same manner, stressing the mindlessness lurking beneath the seemingly meaningful surface of contemporary sayings, even when they are part of Christian ritual, as in the latter example. While these are almost verbatim transcriptions, changed by substituting a few words, and therefore immediately recognizable, Huxley has also generated new synthetic myths in the form of proverbs, e.g., 'One cubic centimetre [of soma] cures ten gloomy sentiments' (*ibid.*, pp. 53, 57, 72), or 'Take a holiday from reality whenever you like, and come back without so much as a headache or a mythology' (*ibid.*, p. 53). Finally, there are pseudostatements, e.g., 'What a hideous colour khaki is' (*ibid.*, p. 58), or 'progress is lovely' (*ibid.*, p. 85), which are somewhat different. As with the jingles and proverbs, a statement is either true or false, i.e., it is possible to establish the conditions under which truth or falsity can be determined When there are no such conditions, the statement becomes meaningless as statement, that is to say, a pseudostatement 'I'm glad I'm not a Gamma' (*ibid.*, p. 59), 'Everybody's happy now' (*ibid.*, pp. 67, 79, 105), or 'Everyone works for everyone else' (*ibid.*, pp. 66, 78), are nether true nor false within the fictional universe. Void of any semantic or logical content, they are meaningless while serving a psychological purpose as consolidators of happiness and security, however vacuous.

These synthetic myths are important for the way in which the fictional universe in *BNW* is experienced by the reader. They are an organic part of the brave new society, as is seen in the deft, almost subliminal manner to which the contemporary pseudostatement 'every man for himself' is rewritten as 'everyone belongs to everyone else', and 'Everyone works for everyone else'. A satirical contrast is established, for not only do people not belong to anybody or anything, they also work for nothing but the senseless perpetuation of society, ending their lives as one and a half kilos of reclaimed phosphorus (*ibid*, p. 66). In this sense, 'Everyone works for everyone else', and 'everyone belongs to everyone else', *mean* 'every man for himself' within the redefined social context. As Bernard Marx discovers, the individual is unalterably alone in spite of his being surrounded with other individuals almost twenty-four hours a day. However, the point is that the synthetic myths to *BNW* are directed, so as not just to cast an ironical sidelight on the ways to which we ourselves use this type of discourse. The horror of Huxley's literal-minded Brave New World is that it *lives* its synthetic myths. Although we are not yet doing thus ourselves, in this 'admonitory satire' Huxley is subtly indicating a potential danger, and giving fair warning.[6] *Brave New World* may have been written by an 'amused, Pyrrhonic aesthete' (*BNW*, p. 8), as Huxley himself pointed out in his 1946 introduction, but it is also an affirmation of Huxley's statement that 'Truth repeated is no longer truth, it becomes truth again only when it has been reaped by the speaker as an immediate experience'.[7] As John Savage, Helmholtz Watson, and Bernard Marx discover, this is the central human predicament.

Notes

2. Ørvad Andersen et al., *Tegneserier En Ekspansionshistorie* (Kongerslev, Denmark GMT 1974), pp. 104–25 contains a detailed and useful discussion of sacred (transempiric) versus modern (popular) myth, as well as the distinction between the analytic and the synthetic myth. These concepts arise out of a closely argued redefinition of Levi-Strauss' transformational theory of myth and lead to a restructured theory of mythic taxonomies.

3. Aldous Huxley, *Brave New World: A Novel* (1932, Harmondsworth: Penguin Books 1955, rpt. 1972). Hereafter cued as *BNW*. Criticism of *BNW* often centers on its anti-utopian aspects, and its relationship towards the utopian/dystopian tradition, especially Yevgeny Zamyatin (*We* 1924) and H. G. Wells, J. O. Bailey, *Pilgrims Through Space and Time: Trends and Patterns to Scientific and Utopian Fiction* (1947, rpt. Westport, Conn.: Greenwood Press, 1972), pp. 155–6, sees *BNW* as an anti-utopian satire, while Mark R. Hillegas in *The Future as Nightmare: H. G. Wells and the Anti-Utopians* (1967, rpt. Carbondale: Southern Ill. University Press, 1974), calls *BNW* an 'admonitory satire' (p. 82) and an 'anti-utopia' (p. 110), but is mostly concerned with its anti-Wellsian aspects (pp. 113, 157, 158). David Ketterer, *New Worlds For Old: The Apocalyptic Imagination, Science Fiction and American Literature* (New York: Doubleday, 1974), emphasizes the dystopian aspect (pp. 100, 125). Frederick W. Conner, 'Attention! Aldous Huxley's Epistemological Route to Salvation', *Sewanee*

Review, LXXXI (1973), 282–308, is not specifically concerned with *BNW*, but rather with Huxley's development as thinker and essayist. However, he does make a point which is important for an understanding of *BNW*'s philosophical context, namely that one of Huxley's central preoccupations was with experience versus abstraction, subjectivism versus objectivity, he indicates that these 'puzzles of epistemology' (p 302) show Huxley 'a way to salvation' (p 302).

4. In this they are reminiscent of the *moralitas* of the medieval beast fable, and in a wider sense the moral of the fairy tale.

5. E.g., 'Winston tastes good, like a cigarette should', 'The right one, the bright one Martini', 'Things go better with Coke'. Once a slogan has been associated with a product, it tends to become even shorter: Martini's slogan has been reduced to 'the right one'. 'Martini' and 'the right one' become synthetic myths which disguise the processes of their mediation. Any specific oppositions which might be mediated by consuming, e.g., Martini have disappeared.

6. Hillegas, *The Future as Nightmare*, p. 82. See above, n. 3.

7. Huxley as quoted by Conner, p. 283. See above, n. 3.

Robert S. Baker on the Evolution of Huxley's Philosophy

In their endeavor to direct the course of history to apparently rational ends, Huxley's World Controllers fostered the development of a society that cherished above all else collective stability and historical stasis. In the novel this revolutionary exercise in control over populations and economic processes had begun after the Nine Years' War, but in actual history, in Soviet Russia—although Huxley insisted that traces of the same processes could be detected in Europe, Great Britain, and North America. Huxley associated such unwelcome developments with the New Romantic fascination with technological progress, and yet the absence of suffering in Mustapha Mond's utopia is attributable to the systematic eradication of precisely those attributes of human nature that Huxley himself found most objectionable. It is this fact that accounts for the curiously ambiguous quality of Huxley's social criticism in *Brave New World*. In this respect, it can be said that

Huxley has created his dystopia in order to frame a complicated question in the guise of an apparently simple juxtaposition of contending points of view. A significant number of Mustapha Mond's principal beliefs, including his repudiation of history, disavowal of the value of the individual ego, dismissal of unlimited historicist progress, rejection of art, and aversion for the family, were shared at this time by Huxley. Indeed, they form the staple subjects of his satirical fiction throughout the interwar period. Mond's political and sociological hypotheses, however, proceed from a corrupted source, one Huxley will explore in greater detail in *Eyeless in Gaza*, while Mond's neurotic quest for absolute material security will reach its psychotic apotheosis in Joseph Stoyte's castle-museum in *After Many a Summer Dies the Swan*. Most important, his consuming passion for a completely regulated society involved an assault on mind and intelligence that Huxley could never countenance.

The secular and material values of the World State represent a massive projection of Lucy Tantamount's insistence in *Point Counter Point* that in the "aeroplane" there is "no room" for "the soul." Just as John the Savage is a variation on Maurice Spandrell, Lenina Crowne is a damped-down version of Lucy Tantamount, shorn of the latter's neuresthenic restiveness and sadomasochistic violence. Like Lucy, Lenina is a fervent admirer of machinery, a believer in progress, and a promiscuous sensualist. To create a secure society for neurotic hedonists like Lucy Tantamount, to purge them of their libidinally destructive drives in an environment of carefully stimulated apathy, is in essence the *raison d'être* of the World State. For Huxley this was a goal of sorts, indeed the only one he could envision for the Europe of the late 1920s. As Mustapha Mond observed, "liberalism ... was dead of anthrax," a casualty of the Nine Years' War.

Huxley associated liberalism with the old romanticism and its stress on individuality, unlimited historical development, and political freedom. Like "history," it is a concept that has no relevance to Fordean paternalism and its monolithic embodiment in the World State. The World Controllers are not presented as charismatic leaders, nor do they require an electoral consensus in order to act. The end of history necessarily implies the death of politics in a world where the rulers have become faceless technocrats, worshipping efficiency and regulation, and administering a complex social system that has no need of ideological justification beyond sleep-taught clichés. Despite these objections to the despotic paternalism of the World Controllers, Huxley permits Mustapha Mond to formulate in the final chapters a detailed apology for Fordean collectivism, including systematic governmental intrusion into and domination of all spheres of human existence. Mond's objections to the psychological and economic anarchy that he believes informs the entire gamut of human history are essentially Huxley's, and his collectivist materialism was if not the most desirable answer to Sadean anarchy, at least a conceivable solution. It should be stressed that the sadistic irrationality Huxley linked with the society of *Point Counter Point* was for the most part a trait of John the Savage, not Mustapha Mond; and while Huxley consistently repudiated Marxist collectivism, he nevertheless observed in a letter written in 1931, approximately two years before the appearance of *Brave New World*, that "the Marxian philosophy of life is not exclusively true: but, my word, it goes a good way, and covers a devil of a lot of ground." A month later he observed in another letter that history was an incurable disease and Marxist economics merely another symptom of social decay: "the human race fills me with a steadily growing dismay. I was staying in the Durham coal-field this autumn, in the heart of English unemployment and it was awful. If only one could believe that the remedies proposed for the awfulness (Communism etc.) weren't even worse than the disease—in fact weren't the disease itself in another form, with superficially different symptoms."

Mond of course is not a Marxist; however, his ideas are similar enough, in the broadest sense, to suggest the scope and depth of the philosophical dilemma in which Huxley found himself in the early thirties. In his next novel, *Eyeless in Gaza*, Huxley will turn to the theme of political engagement—a subject, with the exception of *Point Counter Point*, noticeably absent from the satires of the twenties. Its exigent presence in the world of Maurice Spandrell and Anthony Beavis signals Huxley's departure from the familiar terrain of Eliot's *Waste Land* and his long-postponed incursion into Auden country.

RAFEEQ O. MCGIVERON ON THE LITERARY AND POLITICAL ALLUSIONS BEHIND HUXLEY'S CHOICE OF NAMES

Aldous Huxley's *Brave New World* (1932) "is told with a perfect balance of wit and humor" (Aldiss 185), and an important part of Huxley's wit is his choice of character names, for they subtly support his novel's themes. R. H. Super notes that Huxley's work is "loaded ... with literary allusions ..." (427), and although James Sexton remarks that "all the names Huxley used ... can be traced to actual or literary eponyms" ("Aldous" 85), many do not seem to have been explicated in print. This should be remedied, for with ironic incompatibilities, double meanings, and allusions emphasizing frustrated potential, Huxley's use of names reiterates his warning against the destruction of the individual in the modern world.

One level of Huxley's irony, that of incompatibilities, occurs when his World State invokes the names of leftists such as Marx (35), Engels (80), Trotsky (31), and Bakunin (80) along with the names of prominent historical supporters of capitalism such as the deified Ford, Benito Mussolini (57), Diesel (80), Rothschild (79), Hoover (whether appliance-maker, president, or director of the FBI) (57), and, as Sexton reminds us, the "important industrialist-politician" Alfred Mond ("Aldous" 85; "Rationalization" 429–36). Clearly. such names are incompatible without a strange twisting of ideologies. Rather than taking the best aspects of both capitalist Right and socialist Left, the World State has taken the worst: from the former the subordination of the individual to the supremacy of the collective State, and from the latter the reduction of the individual to compulsive consumer.

References to Rousseau (87), Darwin (260), Napoleon (260), and Habibullah (the pliable pro-British ruler of Afghanistan early in the twentieth century) (87) also contain double meanings. Each name could reflect a positive quality, yet, as is the case with the apparently incompatible names from Left and Right, in Huxley's society each reflects a negative just as easily. The World State values not childlike simplicity but childish hedonism, not scientific inquiry or progress but iron determinism, not idealism or revolutionary vigor but dictatorship, not political prudence but mere complacency.

Just as these state-sanctioned names reflect a society that blithely crushes individuality at every opportunity, the frustrated potentials of specific character names reflect the coopting of individuality. For example, *Darwin Bonaparte*, Bernard *Marx*, *Lenina* Crowne, and *John* the Savage all possess names alluding to rebellion or intellection. All such allusions are ironic, however, their possibilities firmly frustrated by an intellectually stifling society. In addition to these fairly obvious allusions to frustrated potential, Huxley uses others that are rather more subtle or obscure.

Bernard's friend, Helmholtz Watson, is a writer of hypnopaedic propaganda who has begun to realize "that sport, women, communal activities [are] only ... second best" (67). In English *helm* suggests the place of steering or control, whereas in German it means "helmet"; moreover, in German *holtz* means "wooden,"[1] with its connotations of antiquity. This name suits Helmholtz, for like the banned writers of the pre-Fordian era of seven centuries earlier, he is intellectual rather than hedonistic, sensing, "[w]ords can be like X-rays, if you use them properly ..." (70). Unlike the nineteenth-century German scientist Helmholtz, however, he does nothing to advance knowledge. Further, although a wooden helmet may hark back to the freer past, it is also more fragile; though Helmholtz is moved by the linguistic artistry of Shakespeare, the emotional content he finds "irresistibly comical" (188), and his abortive rebellion thus is undermined from its beginning.

A more minor character, Popé, an enemy from John's childhood, also is given a name with unfulfilled potentials.

Whereas the seventeenth-century Popé led a highly successful revolt against the Spanish of New Mexico, the lover of young John's mother is simply a mescal-besotted lecher with braids like sinister "black snake[s]" (134). Though he is named by family and custom on the Savage Reservation rather than by the World State, the irony of his name still reiterates the difficulty of transcending the limitations of a hide-bound society.

The names of Mustapha Mond, the "Resident Controller for Western Europe" (33), reveal unfulfilled potential just as do the others. The reference to the Frenchman Alfred Mond that Sexton notes is straightforward, if now unfortunately obscure, but ironic allusions exist as well. In Arabic mustapha means "the chosen one,"[2] and in French, of course, *monde* means "world." Yet, although Mond is one of the ten most powerful people in the world, to readers he scarcely seems "the chosen one." Although intelligent and inquisitive enough as a young man to risk being exiled, he chose instead to uphold orthodoxy (232–33); he may study his Bible and other banned works (236–37) and may "almost envy" those malcontents he banishes (233), but he wryly supports the system of "[u]niversal happiness [that] keeps the wheels steadily turning" (234). He has kept himself from threatening a world that "prefer[s] to do things comfortably" (247)—without the worries of art, science, or religion (236)—and clearly he will keep others from threatening it as well.

Just as the incompatibilities and double meanings of state-selected names prepare readers for a society that takes the worst of both worlds—whatever they happen to be in any particular allusion—the ironies of the unfulfilled potentials of specific characters' names reiterate the difficulty of freeing the individual from the tyranny of the collective and from the seductions of hedonism. Though many names allude to rebellion and intellection, all characters fail to make any positive change in society, thus reinforcing the more overt themes of *Brave New World*. The grimly witty ironies of Huxley's name choices remind us that only by preserving our humanity and individuality can we avoid the same failure.

Notes

1. I am indebted to Mr. Norbert M. Kurtz, Lead Faculty for Foreign Languages, Lansing Community College, Lansing, Michigan.

2. I am indebted to Mr. John C. Hutchinson of Lansing, Michigan, and Mr. Fuad Al-Kabour of Okemos, Michigan.

Works Cited

Aldiss, Brian W., and David Wingrove. *Trillion Year Spree: The History of Science Fiction*. New York, Atheneum, 1986.

Huxley, Aldous. *Brave New World*, 1932. New York: Harper, 1989.

Sexton, James. "Aldous Huxley's Bokanovsky." *Science-Fiction Studies* 16 (1989): 85–89.

———. "Brave New World and the Rationalization of Industry," *English Studies in Canada* 12 (1986): 424–39.

Super, R. H. "Aldous Huxley's Art of Allusion—The Arnold Connection." *English Studies; A Journal of English Language and Literature* 72 (1991): 426–41.

GUINEVERA A. NANCE ON THE LIMITS OF THE HEROIC

In a society that insists on divorcing sex and emotion, Lenina is well adjusted. It is Bernard who is maladjusted. He is another of Huxley's eccentrics, but, ironically, his peculiarities are those of a sane man. The problem is that he lives in an insane world. His penchant for solitude and his preference for reality over soma-induced unreality make him suspect in this topsy-turvy society that prizes the community more than the individual and happiness more than truth. But the real sign of his unorthodoxy is his interest in cultivating his emotions. Like many of Huxley's characters, Bernard is emotionally infantile; however, in his case it is the result of cultural conditioning and a requirement of social conformity. So when he tells Lenina that he wants "to know what passion is" and "to feel something strongly," he is consciously rebelling against the system that allows some of its subjects to be adults intellectually but requires them to be "infants where feeling and desire are concerned."

Yet for all his brave talk and little acts of defiance, Bernard is not a hero and poses no real challenge to the system. Like Denis Stone, Theodore Gumbril, and other of Huxley's boastful but indecisive protagonists, Bernard is not up to the task of living as "an adult all the time," as he puts it. However, he and his friend Helmholtz Watson, whose superior mental ability also sets him apart, serve a critical function in the first half or so of the novel in being the only dissenters against the order of things.

In addition, Bernard functions as the avenue through which Huxley introduces into the narrative the single perspective that is completely contrary to those prevalent in the World State—the point of view of the Savage, whose unique culture has been concocted from Indian primitivism and Shakespearean sophistication. Once the Savage takes over the role of providing the antithetical perspective, Huxley can largely dispense with Bernard as a dissenting voice. In the last portion of the book, Marx becomes an increasingly unsympathetic character and the object of scathing satire. For example, when his role as guardian of the Savage gives him unprecedented prominence, his dissatisfaction with society dissipates. As the authorial voice of the novel satirically states: "Success went fizzily to Bernard's head, and in the process completely reconciled him ... to a world which, up till then, he had found very unsatisfactory."

Even if Bernard were more inclined to keep up his resistance, he and Helmholtz can only go so far because their conditioning has created boundaries they cannot cross. As Mustapha Mond explains, "each one of us ... goes through life inside a bottle." An Alpha's bottle may be, relatively speaking, enormous, and within it he may have a sense of autonomy; but he still has limits confining him. Only someone from outside the culture and its conditioning can present, if not a challenge, at least a complete contrast. The Savage from the New Mexico reservation represents that contrast. As Peter Firchow observes in his *The End of Utopia*, the appearance of the Savage in the new world "brings about the confrontation of the individual natural man with the artificial society of unnatural men."[5]

Huxley's use of a savage as his principal critic of the civilization crafted through science has the effect of recalling Rousseau's Noble Savage and the whole context of the romantic idealization of the natural man. The reminder turns out to be mostly ironic, however, since Huxley is unprepared to follow the romantic primitivists in asserting the innate goodness of man; nor is he convinced that urbanity is particularly bad. He does share the romantic's suspicion of progress, and it is such a suspicion that prompted the writing of *Brave New World*. But the central irony in Huxley's evocation of the Noble Savage idea is that although John Savage, as he comes to be called, fits the romantic prototype in that he has a natural dignity and intelligence, he is not a savage.

Note

5. Peter Edgerly Firchow, *The End of Utopia: A Study of Aldous Huxley's Brave New World* (Lewisburg: Bucknell University Press, 1984), 89.

MALINDA SNOW ON HUXLEY'S USE OF THOMAS GRAY'S "ELEGY WRITTEN IN A COUNTRY CHURCH YARD"

Readers accustomed to the frequent literary allusions and imitations in Aldous Huxley's prose fiction have probably noticed the parody of the opening of Thomas Gray's "Elegy Written in a Country Church Yard" that begins chapter five of *Brave New World*. (...)

The parody is easily discerned. Like Gray, Huxley describes a twilight scene with people heading homeward; the setting is the Stoke Poges Golf Club. Gray's "glimmering landscape" has only one human figure, the plowman, while Huxley's "fading landscape" has many human figures, including the herd-like lower-caste golfers. The "lowing herd" of the poem moves purposefully, while the "lowing" cattle of *Brave New World* are unseen in the "Internal and External Secretion Trust." Gray's curfew bell is replaced in *Brave New World* by loudspeakers, his "drowsy tinklings" from the sheepfold by the bells of trams, his "droning" flight of beetles by "an incessant buzzing of helicopters," his church tower by the clubhouse tower. And instead of Gray's elegant verse, there is Huxley's deliberately commonplace prose.

The essence of meaning in Huxley's novel lies in comparisons: past and future, emotion and sensation, pain and pleasure, nature and the unnatural, the rational and the irrational. As the reader recalls more and more of the "Elegy," he realizes that all which Gray celebrates is twisted or negated in the "brave new world." Every value that Gray affirms has become a vice in Huxley's "future" civilization.[2] The sources of pleasure noted by Gray include family affection, modest work, and solitary reflection. They offer happiness to those who accept man's position in the natural order of things and accept his mutability. Huxley's *Brave New World*, on the other hand, presents a society that ignores man's weaknesses and the ultimate defeat of death. The pleasures of family life, in which one loves other people and recognizes one's position in a cyclical pattern of birth and death, are denied to citizens in the year of Our Ford 632. Another source of pleasure, the "useful toil" to which Gray accords the tribute of notice, serves in the "Elegy" as an emblem of the individual's dignity and independence. In *Brave New World*, such mottoes as "even Epsilons are useful" signal only isolation and anonymity. The amalgamation of the individual into the social structure of the novel is accomplished by denying him specific recognition and also the pleasure of withdrawal and reflection, precisely the pleasures acknowledged by Gray's speaker.

The "Elegy" is the most famous of many eighteenth-century reflective poems in which the speaker is a solitary individual who withdraws from society to ponder his place in it. This situation is beautifully sketched in the opening lines of the poem, and the reader soon realizes that it is the integrity and privacy of the rural man that the speaker most admires as he reflects on the darkening landscape

> Far from the madding crowd's ignoble strife,
> Their sober wishes never learn'd to stray,
> Along the cool sequester'd vale of life
> They kept the noiseless tenor of their way[3]

Huxley makes a neat parody of "the noiseless tenor" in his description of the Stroke Poges Golf Course, where loudspeakers begin "in a more than human tenor, to announce the closing of the courses."[4] The loudspeakers and other mechanical means of imposing society's norms on the individual remind us that privacy and reflection are not possible in the "brave new world." The citizen is conditioned to fear being alone and being out-of-doors in a natural setting: "A love of nature keeps no factories busy It was decided to abolish the love of nature" (16). A starry night is "on the whole depressing" (58), and Lenina Crowne is frightened by the view of moonlight on the sea that the "strange" Bernard Marx finds so attractive. The failure of Bernard, and of John the Savage, to fit into the social structure of the novel derives in part from their need for privacy and reflection outside that structure. (...)

There is no character in Huxley's novel who, as a visitor from the past, observes the future society and fully perceives the disparity between man's real place and the view of that place presented in the narrative. According to Ellen Douglass Leyburn this fact significantly affects the position and function of the reader of the satire: Huxley is "willing to dispense with the dreamer from our day who is transported into the new world. The dreamer is perforce the reader...."[6] Huxley's parody of Gray's lines enhances the reader's role as "dreamer," for it reminds him of comparisons he must make in order to feel the novel's satire in all its sharpness. The "Elegy" is a familiar source of ideas to readers; conscious of the parody, they will see the ideological relationships between the poem and the novel. In order to succeed, satire must have as its basis a recognizable set of values that the institution being satirized either lacks or violates. The parody of Gray's "Elegy" in *Brave New World* serves the satire by reminding the reader of specific concepts he values and finds missing in the society Huxley describes.

Notes

2. Huxley's "future" world is, of course, a satirical view of the present, an automated, synthetic world quite different from the pastoral scenes Gray describes. Peter Firchow ("The Satire of Huxley's *Brave New World*," *Modern Fiction Studies* 12 [1966] 451–60), suggests that the society in the novel is based on what Huxley saw during a visit to Los Angeles in the 1920s.

3. "Elegy Written in a Country Church Yard," ll. 73–76, *The Complete Poems of Thomas Gray: English, Latin, and Greek*, ed. H. W. Starr and J. R. Hendrickson (Oxford, 1966). Future references to "Elegy" are cited by line in the text.

4. *Brave New World and Brave New World Revisited* (New York, 1965), p. 56. Future references are from this edition and are cited by page in the text.

6. *Satiric Allegory: Mirror of Man* (New Haven, 1956), p. 115.

Works by Aldous Huxley

Novels

Crome Yellow, 1921.

Mortal Coils, 1922.

Antic Hay, 1923.

Young Archimedes, 1924.

Those Barren Leaves, 1925.

Point Counter Point, 1928.

Leda, 1929.

The World of Light, 1931.

Brave New World, 1932.

Jesting Pilate: The Diary of a Journey, 1932.

Eyeless in Gaza, 1936.

The Perennial Philosophy, 1938.

After Many a Summer Dies the Swan, 1939.

Time Must Have a Stop, 1944.

Ape and Essence, 1948.

The Devils of Loudon, 1952.

The Doors of Perception, 1954.

Genius and Goddess, 1955.

Heaven and Hell, 1956.

After the Fireworks, 1957.

Brave New World Revisited, 1958.

Island, 1962.

The Crows of Pearblossom, 1967.

Jacob's Hands, with Christopher Isherwood, 1998.

Collections

The Burning Wheel: Poems, 1916.

The Defeat of Youth: And Other Poems, 1918.

Limbo, 1918.

Selected Poems, 1925.

Two or Three Graces: And Other Stories, 1926.

Arabia Infelix and Other Poems, 1929.

Do What You Will, 1929.

Brief Candles, 1930.

The Cicadas: And Other Poems, 1931.

Rotunda: A Selection of His Work, 1932.

Texts and Pretexts, 1933.

The Olive Tree: And Other Essays, 1936.

Ends and Means, 1937.

Brave New World and Brave New World Revisited, 1942.

Stories, Essays and Poems, 1942.

Little Mexican: Six Stories, 1948.

Themes and Variations, 1950.

Tomorrow and Tomorrow and Tomorrow: And Other Essays, 1956.

The Art of Seeing, 1957.

The Collected Poetry of Aldous Huxley, 1971.

The World of Aldous Huxley: An Omnibus of His Fiction and Non-Fiction Over Three Decades, 1971.

The Doors of Perception and Heaven and Hell: Vol. 1, 1972.

Non-fiction

On the Margin, 1923.

Along the Road: Notes and Essays of a Tourist, 1925.

Essays New and Old, 1926.

Proper Studies, 1928.

Holy Face and Other Essays, 1929.

Vulgarity in Literature: Digressions from a Theme, 1930.

The Letters of D. H. Lawrence, 1932.

Beyond the Mexique Bay, 1934.

The Elder Peter Breugel 1528(?)–1569, with Jean Videpoche 1938.

Grey Eminence: A Study in Religion and Politics, 1941.

Science, Liberty and Peace, 1946.

ADONIS and The Alphabet: and Other Essays, 1956.

On Art and Artists, 1960.

Aldous Huxley: A Collection of Critical Essays, 1968.

Letters of Aldous Huxley, 1969.

Moksha: Aldous Huxley's Classic Writings on Psychedelics and the Visionary Experience 1931–1963, 1980.

Complete Essays, Volume 3 1930–1935, 2000.

Short Stories

"The Gioconda Smile," 1922.

"Two or Three Graces," 1926.

"The Dwarfs"

"Young Archimedes"

Annotated Bibliography

Atkins, John. *Aldous Huxley: A Literary Study*. London: Calder, 1956; revised, London: Calder & Boyars, 1967; New York: Orion Press, 1968.

Atkins's proves to be one of the first comprehensive studies on the life and work of Aldous Huxley.

Baker, Robert S. *Brave New World: History, Science, and Dystopia*. Boston: Twayne, 1990.

In this volume, Robert S. Baker discusses the political implications of *Brave New World*, and its relevance to the twentieth century.

Baker, Robert S. *The Dark Historic Page: Social Satire and Historicism in the Novels of Aldous Huxley 1921–1939*. Madison: University of Wisconsin Press, 1982.

In this study, Baker investigates the role of Darwinism and scientific progression as the historical backdrop for Huxley's futuristic novel.

Birnbaum, Milton. *Aldous Huxley's Quest for Values*. Knoxville: University of Tennessee Press, 1971.

Birnbaum's book is a serious consideration of Huxley's views on religion and spirituality. Of specific interest are the discussions on the various "diseases" Huxley considered to be plaguing mankind.

Bowering, Peter. *Aldous Huxley: A Study of the Major Novels*. New York: Oxford UP, 1969.

A comprehensive study of Huxley's major novels, with a chapter focusing on *Brave New World*, and in particular, it's themes of technological slavery and limitations on personal freedom.

Bradshaw, David. *The Hidden Huxley*. London: Faber & Faber, 1994.

This volume contains a collection of Huxley's insights and opinions on the issues of his time and tries to argue for a distinct evolution in Huxley's thinking.

Deery, June. *Aldous Huxley and the Mysticism of Science*. New York: St. Martin's Press, 1996.

Deery analyzes Huxley's use and knowledge of science as he applied it to literary fiction. This volume also traces Huxley's influence on popular culture, and how he has contributed to interdisciplinary debates on religion, literature, and science.

Firchow, Peter. *Aldous Huxley: Satirist and Novelist*. Minneapolis: University of Minnesota Press, 1972.

In this study, Firchow traces the development of Huxley's use of satire in his writing, from Huxley's early short stories and poems to his later novels.

Firchow, Peter. *The End of Utopia: A Study of Aldous Huxley's Brave New World*. Lewisburg: Bucknell UP, 1984.

Firchow discusses his interpretation of *Brave New World's* assessment of the future, and reflects on the questions Huxley raises in the novel.

Grushow, Ira. "Brave New World and The Tempest." *College English* 24, no. 1 (Oct., 1962), 42–45.

In this essay, Grushow examines the relationship between Shakespeare's play and Huxley's novel, particularly regarding John the Savage's displacement in the "brave new world."

Holmes, Charles M. *Aldous Huxley and the Way to Reality*. Bloomington: Indiana UP, 1969.

Holmes traces Huxley's path for reality and its impact on his novels, and addresses Huxley's interpretations of the mystical and visionary.

Larsen, Peter M. "Synthetic Myths in Aldous Huxley's *Brave New World* A Note." *English Studies* 62 (1981): 506–508.

In this essay, Larsen defines the synthetic myth and discusses its importance to the "fictional universe" of *Brave New World*.

McGiveron, Rafeeq O. "Huxley's *Brave New World*." *The Explicator* 57, Issue 1 (Fall 1998): 27. 4p.

McGiveron examines Huxley's use of ironic allusion with respect to the names of the characters in *Brave New World*. He discusses the double meanings and political and literary implications of the characters' names.

Meckier, Jerome. *Aldous Huxley: Satire and Structure*. New York: Barnes & Noble, 1971.

Jerome Meckier explores Huxley's major satiric themes and analyzes the novelistic forms desired to present them. This fusion of satire and structure is traced through the early novels to the Utopian concerns of the later ones. There is an account of the Huxley-D.H. Lawrence relationship and a discussion of counterpoint.

Nance, Guinevera A. *Aldous Huxley*. New York: Continuum, 1988.

Nance devotes a chapter on *Brave New World*, providing summary and critical analysis, with an emphasis on the moral implications of the Savage.

Snow, Malinda. "The Grey Parody in *Brave New World*." *Papers on Language and Literature* 13 (1977): 85–88.

In this essay, Snow discusses how Huxley's use of Thomas Gray's "Elegy Written in a Country Church Yard" sharpens the reader's understanding of Huxley's satirical intent in the novel.

Watt, Donald, ed. *Aldous Huxley: The Critical Heritage*. London: Routledge & Kegan Paul, 1975.

A collection of notable book reviews and critical essays on the works of Aldous Huxley.

Watts, Harold H. *Aldous Huxley*. New York: Twayne, 1969.

Watts discusses *Brave New World* as dystopian fiction, and examines its structures, characterizations, and themes.

Woodcock, George. *Dawn and the Darkest Hour: A Study of Aldous Huxley*. New York: Viking, 1972.

Woodcock's intellectual biography examines the many facets of Aldous Huxley, as a novelist, artist, and moralist, to name a few.

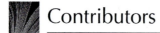# Contributors

Harold Bloom is Sterling Professor of the Humanities at Yale University and Henry W. and Albert A. Berg Professor of English at the New York University Graduate School. He is the author of over 20 books, including *Shelley's Mythmaking* (1959), *The Visionary Company* (1961), *Blake's Apocalypse* (1963), *Yeats* (1970), *A Map of Misreading* (1975), *Kabbalah and Criticism* (1975), *Agon: Toward a Theory of Revisionism* (1982), *The American Religion* (1992), *The Western Canon* (1994), and *Omens of Millennium: The Gnosis of Angels, Dreams, and Resurrection* (1996). *The Anxiety of Influence* (1973) sets forth Professor Bloom's provocative theory of the literary relationships between the great writers and their predecessors. His most recent books include *Shakespeare: The Invention of the Human* (1998), a 1998 National Book Award finalist, *How to Read and Why* (2000), *Genius: A Mosaic of One Hundred Exemplary Creative Minds* (2002), and *Hamlet: Poem Unlimited* (2003). In 1999, Professor Bloom received the prestigious American Academy of Arts and Letters Gold Medal for Criticism, and in 2002 he received the Catalonia International Prize.

Aislinn Goodman has graduated from Yale University in 2002, and resides in Atlanta. She is also the author of *Bloom's Major Novelists: Edith Wharton*.

Peter Bowering is a respected essayist and academic. His published work includes *Aldous Huxley: a Study of the Major Novels*.

Jerome Meckier is a Professor of English at the University of Kentucky, whose published work includes *Aldous Huxley: Satire and Structure* and books on Victorian Literature.

Laurence Brander is the author of *Aldous Huxley: A Critical Study*, and *George Orwell*.

Peter Firchow has been an active educator and critic. He is the author of *Aldous Huxley: Satirist and Novelist* and *The End of Utopia: A Study of Aldous Huxley's* Brave New World.

Ira Grushow is Alumni Professor of English Belles Lettres and Literature Department at Franklin & Marshall College. He is the author of *The Imaginary Reminiscences of Sir Max Beerbohm*.

Peter M. Larsen is the author of "Synthetic Myths in Aldous Huxley's *Brave New World* A Note."

Robert S. Baker has been a Professor of English at the University of Wisconsin at Madison. He is the author of *The Dark Historic Page: Social Satire and Historicism in the Novels of Aldous Huxley, 1921–1939* and *Brave New World: History, Science, and Dystopia*.

Rafeeq O. McGiveron has published articles in *The Explicator*, *Western American Literature*, and *Extrapolation*.

Guinevera A. Nance is a member of the English Department and Chancellor of Auburn University Montgomery. She has written books on Aldous Huxley, Philip Roth, and others.

Malinda Snow is Associate Professor of English at Georgia State University. She has published articles on eighteenth century literature.

Acknowledgments

Aldous Huxley: A Critical Study of the Major Novels by Peter Bowering: 102–104. © 1969 by Oxford University Press. Reprinted by permission.

Aldous Huxley: Satire and Structure by Jerome Meckier: 176–78. © 1969 by Jerome Meckier. Published by Chatto & Windus. Reprinted by permission of the author.

Aldous Huxley: A Critical Study by Laurence Brander: 67–69. © 1970 by Bucknell University Press. Reprinted with permission of Bucknell University Press.

"The American Dream: *Brave New World* and *Ape* and *Essence*" by Peter Firchow. From *The End of Utopia: A Study of Aldous Huxley's Brave New World*: 119–122. © 1984 by Bucknell University Press. Reprinted by permission.

"Brave New World and The Tempest" by Ira Grushow. From *College English* 24:1 (October 1962): 42–45. © 1962 by Ira Grushow. Reprinted by permission of the author.

"Synthetic Myths in Aldous Huxley's *Brave New World* A Note" by Peter M. Larsen. From *English Studies* 62: 506–8. © 1981 English Studies. Reprinted by permission.

The Dark Historic Page: Social Satire and Historicism in the Novels of Aldous Huxley 1921–1939 by Robert S. Baker: 143–45. © 1982 by University of Wisconsin Press. Reprinted by permission.

"Heaven and Hell: The Utopian Theme in Three Novels" by Guinevera A. Nance. From *Aldous Huxley*: 74–76. © 1988 by Guinevere A. Nance. Reprinted by permission of Continuum Publishing.

"The Gray Parody in *Brave New World*" by Malinda Snow. From *Papers on Language and Literature* 13: 85–88. © 1977 by Papers on Language and Literature. Reprinted by permission.

Index